D1236336

LOSING THE HATE

SIMON PALMER

Simon Palmer

Losing the Hate

Published by Youwriteon.com, 2011
Copyright ©Simon Palmer
First Edition

The author has asserted their moral right under the Copyright, Designs and Patents Act, 1988, to be identified as the author of this work.

All Rights reserved. No part of this publication may be reproduced, copied, stored in a retrieval system, or transmitted, in any form or by any means, without the prior written consent of the copyright holder, nor be otherwise circulated in any form of binding or cover other than that in which it is published and without a similar condition being imposed on the subsequent purchaser.

A CIP catalogue record for this title is available from the British Library.

Simon Palmer

"Holding onto anger is like grasping a hot coal with the intent of throwing it at someone else; you are the one who gets burned."

Siddhartha Gautama

Simon Palmer

I'd like to thank Claudia for being my rock during the editing of this book, and for her invaluable advice· She put a lot of hours of her own time into it for me, and I will be forever thankful·

Thank you to Peter Strange, for the cover photograph, and his continued support of, Losing the Hate·

Simon Palmer

FORWARD BY CLAUDIA B. MODIE
(AUTHOR OF HYBRID)

As a mother of three boys, I have experienced the impulse to lull myself into a false sense of security with regards to sexual abuse. After all, it's girls who are most at risk right?

Statistically this appears to be the case; however, since boys are less likely to tell, these statistics are somewhat skewed and far from reliable.

The sad fact is our children, regardless of sex, are being exploited. It happens in our places of worship, our schools, and most disturbingly in our very own homes.

No amount of money, physical location or parental vigilance for that matter, can shield us from the predators lurking in the human jungle. These hunters are not motivated by survival; they prey on our children merely to satisfy their own perversions. And until we declare open season on these vile sub-humans, our children will remain at risk.

I came across Losing the Hate, on a website which enables writer's to critique one another. As is common, I planned on reading a few chapters, making my comments, and moving on. Instead, I read it in one afternoon, only setting it down when it was absolutely necessary.

Never having experienced such an emotional reaction to a book, my need to reach out to the author became a compulsion, and I acted on my instincts. We became fast friends, and despite his living in England and my residing in America, not a day has passed since without our speaking. The Atlantic has only managed to separate us in a physical sense.

I only mention this because, other than the seven years it took Sye to write Losing the Hate, I have been privileged to share his journey in the evolution of this work.

There have been many frustrations on the road to getting the book to its present state, primarily because it is difficult for Sye to re-visit the horrific events of his past, but there have also been other emotional issues to contend with.

Not long before publication, Sye received a critique in which another author accused him of having "enjoyed" his abuse, even going on to say, "he was just afraid to admit it." These comments were made by a woman who wrote a memoir on her experiences with incest. And although her words were hurtful and ignorant, they did serve to clarify the importance of bringing this book to print.

If these attitudes are so deeply ingrained that even victims of sexual abuse "blame the victim," belittling their suffering based on gender, it only serves to perpetuate continued abuse.

In fact, we may inadvertently be placing our male children at greater risk by making them a more appealing target. Especially when the likelihood of being found out is lessened by the stigma attached to the admission.

[10]

We have to allow boys to feel they will be equally supported in these appalling circumstances.

Men have to be encouraged to speak out without being accused of "enjoying it," or for fear of being falsely labeled homosexual.

I am extremely proud of Sye for having the courage to make **Losing the Hate** public.

Simon Palmer

INTRODUCTION

I've often thought of putting the story of my child abuse into words, usually after about twelve pints of lager or a few bottles of cheap red wine. But inevitably the pain surfaces; and what starts out as a gentle breeze always manages to transform into a formidable storm, one which has haunted me for many years.

My head feels as though it's going to burst when this happens; and without thinking I hurt my loved ones by subconsciously trying to drive them away, often by verbally abusing them. And at times, when the need to lash out overcomes me, I have threatened them physically; adding yet another layer of guilt to my already overburdened sense of self-worth.

You see . . . dear old Simon has always been too ashamed to confide in anyone. And I can honestly say I'm not sure if it's the judgment, or the pity I have convinced myself would be forthcoming that frightens me most. Be that as it may; I have decided my silence has done more harm than good . . . both in my past and in my present existence.

I am beginning this journey with a heavy heart, and my soul is absolutely exhausted, but I have come to the realisation that the shame I have shouldered throughout my life, was never mine to carry.

[13]

Whatever sadness I feel is not so much a result of the experiences; it stems primarily from the knowledge that there are monsters living among us. And although I have managed to gain some perspective on the shame, it is the guilt which continues to eat away at me.

Intellectually I know when I berate myself for not exposing these animals; I am looking back at the situation from an adult capacity. The thought that other children might fall prey to these monsters and suffer the same fate did not even occur to me at the time. But it's this thought that now gnaws at me almost constantly. It is in this spirit that I choose to break my silence, lay the shame where it belongs, and get on with my life.

Although the self harming hasn't happened for many years, it is very much swimming within the deepest recesses of my mind, waiting with bated breath; ready to pounce in any given explosive situation. I sometimes feel it would be easier to tame a wild animal than to suppress those terrifying urges, urges that appear so determined to retake control of my life.

In the forty one years I've been alive, and in the thirty one years my whole body has been burdened with emotional pain; I have never cut myself because I've truly wanted to die, or used it as a desperate cry for help. The act of a running razor blade across my forearm has never caused me any pain.

In fact, when the dark red blood has flowed from my wounds, it has always been the hurt, the fear, and the anguish that have escaped, if only temporarily.

It seems whenever my life is just starting to work itself out, my demons erupt from the swirling dark mist contained inside my head and tear everything to pieces. Silent screams of hate pound my eardrums and turn love into a dangling carrot that becomes just out of my grasp.

Its time to confront my demons head on, and hopefully break the solid foundations that have cemented them inside me for so many gut wrenching years. For far too long I've been afraid to trust anyone, fearing that letting someone into the space surrounding me will enable them to steal what's left of my identity.

I would like dedicate this book to everyone who has inadvertently been on the receiving end of the more trying times of my life, but most of all, it's for my parents.

Simon Palmer

For Mum and Dad

Simon Palmer

PART ONE:
MEETING A MONSTER

Simon Palmer

THE BEGINNING

You can imagine the excitement I felt when, at the age of ten, a highly thought of and well respected teacher at my school asked if I would like to be included in a photographic project which was due to be displayed as part of the forthcoming parents' evening. I was completely overjoyed. The teacher, Mr. Ropeman, explained that he would need to gain permission from my Mother or Father, saying it would be more convenient if the shots were taken on a Saturday morning. And so it was arranged; I would meet him outside the staff room at the end of the school day.

As the afternoon drew to a close I could think of nothing else. Perhaps if the photos were good enough it would be possible for me to do some more. I liked this teacher, and felt as honoured as any child of that age would.

After a lot of clock watching, the final bell sounded and as soon as my class was dismissed I made my way towards the staff room, eagerness coursing through my veins. I pushed against the throng of children desperately trying to escape the clutches of school, as if it were some kind of terrifying monster, when all the time it was myself who was getting ever closer to a monster; a creature more scary than any child could possibly dream of.

Ropeman led me to his car and we drove the short distance to my home where he had a brief conversation with my Mother, who agreed that the proposed "photo shoot" would be perfectly fine. She even asked him if he would let her have a couple of copies for the family album.

Once he left, I hurried into the back garden, silently playing and keeping an eye out for my Father to arrive home from work. I couldn't wait to share my news and tell him of the adventure I was about to embark on.

I knew he would be excited for me, and it wouldn't matter if he'd had a hard day at work; it never did. He was always there for me, always ready with an enthusiastic smile. Even when all he wanted was to sit and relax, one look at my outstretched arms as I ran in his direction immediately brought my father to his knees. However weary he may have felt, there was always time for a hug. I have vivid memories of him swinging me around and around, laughing as he did so. My mother was usually not far off, love almost oozing from every pore of her body as she watched our frolicking about.

My life started with them at the age of five months. They loved children so much that they became foster parents for the local authority, looking after babies whilst their own parents dealt with the various problems life had unwittingly thrown at them. Thankfully, I was one of those babies.

My stay with them was initially meant to be short term, typically no longer than a three month period, while my natural Mother finished a short spell in prison (my place of birth). The plan was that once she was rehabilitated, I would stay with her for weekends, and eventually move back on a permanent basis.

However, following my Mother's continued back slides, and her inability to take parenthood seriously, the social workers decided that the best course of action would be to put me up for adoption. In the mean time, Maureen and Les Palmer agreed to care for me until the time a suitable family was found.

Unbeknown to me, the Palmers had applied to adopt me themselves, wanting to give me a stable family life as one of their own. And so, during the summer of 1972, I became the son they never had, Simon James Palmer.

Suddenly my young world completely changed. I went from being in care to having the perfect Parents, together with three doting sisters. The entire family, my family, including aunts and uncles, never treated me as an outsider and everyone automatically loved me with a passion that was almost indescribable.

Every Saturday we'd visit my Mother's sister, Kitty, and her husband John. These visits were always a big affair, with most of their nine children also spending the day with them. My Dad would sit in the kitchen playing cards with Uncle John, while Mum sat in the lounge watching television and having a laugh. It was a wonderful time, and I have many fond memories of those days.

Dad worked very hard as a lorry driver, often taking me along during the school holidays, while Mum did a fantastic job as a housewife, running the home to the best of her ability. There was always enough money for meals, seaside breaks, and the most fantastic Christmas's any child could possibly wish for. All in all, they were, and will remain, in my heart, the best people in the entire world.

On that fateful day when Ropeman appeared on their doorstep, my Mother and Father, possibly the most attentive parents ever put on this earth, were conned and manipulated by a very clever and sinister man. They were duped, tricked into allowing their only son to be exploited within the perverse world of child pornography.

The events which were about to unfold would change the course of everyone's lives.

THE PHOTO SHOOT

The next day at school Ropeman asked me if the following Saturday would be okay to take the photographs. I said that'd be great and excitedly ranted about how much I was looking forward to doing them. He patted me on the shoulder and smiled, saying that if at all possible I should bring a few items of clothing. When I asked what it was I should wear, he simply replied, "Whatever you look good in."

After what seemed to be an absolute lifetime, Saturday morning finally arrived and I was ready and waiting outside the school gates, clutching a carrier bag my Mother had filled with various items of clothing. It was only a matter of minutes before Ropeman pulled up in his car, beaming his usual smile and gesturing for me to get into the front seat, "Morning young man, you all set and raring to go then?"

"You bet," I answered, "I got some jeans an' T-shirts, Mum ironed me school uniform an' all."

"Excellent, lets rock an' roll then." He seemed to be as excited as I was, explaining that we would be doing the shoot at his flat, saying it made more sense since his equipment was stored there.

The drive only took about twenty minutes, and as I got out of the car an unfamiliar sound of gravel crunched under my feet. A huge Victorian house seemed to peer down, almost beckoning me with it's large "window-eyes," inviting me to enter it's mouth; and as I continued to gaze at the sheer magnitude of the building I felt his hand rest on my shoulder, "It's not all mine I'm afraid."

When I looked up at Ropeman, I noticed he was almost beaming, a smile plastered across his chubby face. Without hesitating I smiled too, still feeling fortunate and tremendously excited.

We walked side by side across the drive, up the enormous stone steps and entered the gigantic front door. Any onlooker who may have happened to glance our way could easily have mistaken us for Father and Son.

Inside was a rather unexpectedly small hallway with a winding staircase leading up to the first floor. Ropeman gestured me towards an inner door opposite the stairs. He led me down a narrow passageway that opened out into an impressive lounge. The room was littered with bookcases, but my eyes were immediately drawn to the lighting and tripod that dominated the centre of the living space. Ropeman left me alone while he sorted out some cold drinks. When he returned I could hardly believe my eyes; he was carrying two glasses of beer. I put the glass to my lips and took a huge mouthful.

"You take your time with that young man; there'll be hell to pay if I take you home tidily."

I was ten years old.

He suggested that we begin straight away and I was told to sit on the sofa, ignoring the camera as best as my excitement would allow. Maybe about six or seven shots were taken when, as cheerful as ever, Ropeman asked me to take off my top. He explained that it would add to the image of me relaxing at home.

The request made me feel quite embarrassed, but ignoring the sudden wave of apprehension sweeping over me, I agreed and removed my T-shirt.

A dozen or so more pictures were taken before we took a short break. He offered me more beer. We chatted about school and what I got up to during the evening with my friends, Peter Simpson and Mark Milner. They were also his students, and the thought crossed my mind how envious they would be when they found out I had spent the day at Ropeman's home, drinking beer no less..

Once the small talk was all but done he piped up with what was quite obviously the next part of his elaborate plan, "What do you think of stretching out on the sofa, as if you were asleep? Think you can do that?"

"Yeah, be easy," I said with false bravado as another wave of apprehension took hold.

And it was there, as I lay on the settee that my journey into hell began.

[27]

Simon Palmer

I remember feeling as though a thousand eyes were staring at me; and at that moment I truly hated the camera more than anything in the entire world.

When Ropeman instructed me to pull my jeans up as far as they would go, my young mind had no idea that the next shot would be centered on my private parts.

Minutes later my photo was being taken with me wearing nothing but my underpants, again, pulled up as far as they would go.

Take it away, take it away,

Smash it or burn it, that Saturday·

Tear it and rip it,

Take the memory away,

I long to forget that Saturday·

Leave me, leave me, and leave me alone,

No more photos, just take me home·

Don't give me smiles,

An' I don't want your beer,

Don't ask me to strip,

Don't fill me with fear·

I hate you, I hate you·

You horrible man·

I often wonder how many lives may have been destroyed by my silence, how many tears were shed because I did not have the strength to tell anyone what he'd done to me?

Sometimes, when my mind travels back to those horrific years, reliving the anguish and torment, desperately trying to understand why he did those things, I wonder if my fear of speaking out indirectly sealed another child's fate. When, stripped to the waist, while standing in the middle of his lounge with nothing but my briefs on, was I helping to lay the blueprints of someone else's future? Sealing another young person's nightmare at the hands of a vile and twisted creature?

I know that in the cold light of day, I'm in no way to blame for anything, but it doesn't stop me from feeling these emotions.

God, how I wish that my silence hadn't been quite so damned silent.

While Ropeman was driving me home, which was around lunchtime, he expressed how successful the morning had been, but asked me to keep it to myself, telling me that he didn't want the surprise for the parent evening being spoilt.

When I asked if we needed to do any more, he winked at me, "It certainly wouldn't do any harm to have another session."

My heart sank.

The car pulled up a couple of hundred yards away from my house and quite unexpectedly, Ropeman thrust a ten pound note into my hand.

Putting the cash into my pocket, it never occurred to me that I was going to have to lie to Mum and Dad, or conceal the money completely. As if reading my mind, the last words that Ropeman said to me that afternoon were, "Tell you what, the money and the beer, that'll be our little secret too."

I nodded in agreement and got out of the car.

Had I not remained silent, the cash would have added concrete to my claim, enforcing the fact that he was trying to bribe me into keeping tight lipped about his "grooming procedure." At the time I really didn't need to think about what I was going to do; there was absolutely no way I was brave enough to mention any of this to my family, and besides, he hadn't hurt me . . . had he?

Saturday afternoons always saw my parents and me visiting my Aunt and Uncle, where my father would enjoy an evening of cribbage whilst my Mother sat in the lounge nattering with her sister, Kitty. They lived on the notorious North Peckham estate, which was only a half an hour drive from our house. It was through the course of the journey that I intended to tell Mum and Dad my first lie.

As the car roared into life and we drove away from our house, my Mother asked how the morning with Mr. Ropeman had gone. Knowing that this was my chance to tell her what had happened, and aware that I didn't need any proof in the eyes of my parents, I simply replied, "Yeah it was really good. He said that I did well too. I think he wants me to do some more for the display too, get some real goodens."

"Good, did you meet his wife as well?" enquired my Mum.

"I, I don't think he's married. It was just him and me today."

My whole body felt as though it was suddenly being consumed by the back seat of the car, like some grotesque alien was intent on devouring me. Or had that been this morning?

In any case, without thinking the lie flew from my lips, "D'you know me mate at school, Trevor? Trevor Goddard?"

"How much?" interjected my Father.

"No, no it's nothing like that! I forgot to tell you yesterday! He said I can go to his house for tea on Monday! Can I go? Please?"

By the time I'd finished the lie, I was sitting forward in my seat like a dog expecting a bone, "Please, can I?"

It was decided I could go.

After school on Monday afternoon I walked to the local railway station and purchased a return ticket to London Bridge. I hovered around the entrance to the London Dungeon for about half an hour, but decided not to try and get in. I bought some sweets from a newsagents instead . . . for the train ride home. Once back in my own area, I took a gentle stroll to my friend Peter's house and asked him to look after the rest of the money for me, telling him I'd stolen it from my Mum's rent tin.

Yet another lie.

[31]

Simon Palmer

THE TEXAS CHAINSAW MASSACRE

By the third week of the summer holidays boredom had well and truly set in; and there was nothing exciting to do. It had been a good few months since my encounter with Ropeman and thankfully the second installment of the photo shoot had not as yet taken place. I'm not sure if my mind blocked it out, but with no conscious strain, I hadn't really thought about it for ages, and it certainly didn't appear to be bothering me anymore.

One particular afternoon was dominated with an intense heat from what was proving to be a fantastic summer. I'd just left Peter's house following a slight disagreement about nothing of any great importance. Truth be told, I can't really remember what it was about.

Deciding to go in search of Mark Milner, I made my way down the road towards the local park, when passing my school, which should have been locked up until September; my eye caught some movement in the small staff car park. Once I was a   bit closer the figure on the other side of the gates looked up and smiled at me.

It was Ropeman. Immediately and without warning, all of the fear I'd experience on that fateful morning came bubbling to the surface, and my head felt as though it was going to explode any minute. Images came flooding into my mind; spinning and swirling, hurting.

The monster said hello and asked me how the holiday was going so far. I told him that it was all getting a bit boring, and looking to the ground, was about to say goodbye when he offered me a lift home. The question truly frightened me and feeling too scared to say no, I nodded my head in acceptance. Ropeman locked the gates and we walked across the road where his car was parked.

Why does your smile,

Fill me with fear?

I'm not back at school,

So why are you here?

I don't want to be,

Here in your car,

Give me an island,

That's distant and far·

I want to play football,

And swing in the park,
I don't want to feel,
Alone in the dark·
I wish I could tell,
My Mum what you've done,
Then I could go back,
To fun in the sun·
But, I'm still here,
In the seat of your car,
Trapped,
Like a frog in a jar·
Where should I look?
What should I say?
Will you take me to hell?
Or use me for play?
I cannot contain,
All this fear in my head,
How nice it would be,
To lay dead in my bed·
It's got to be better,
Than here in your car·

Once in the car Ropeman bombarded me with questions. And although I can't really remember all of them, the following is a rough account of that conversation.

ROPEMAN: I expect you'll be meeting up with your friends later?

SIMON: Nope.

ROPEMAN: You've not got any plans for the rest of the day then?

SIMON: Dunno, just hang around an' get bored I s'pose.

ROPEMAN: I'm not doing much myself. I was toying with the idea of renting a movie, how'd you like to join me? You can choose it if you like.

SIMON: I, I dunno, what about me Mum? She might tell me off.

ROPEMAN: Well I'm sure she wouldn't mind, but we don't have to tell her, it could be one of our little secrets, what do you think? It'd only be for a couple of hours.

The only answer I managed to push through my lips was the one he wanted to hear; I said yes. Turning the car around, Ropeman headed towards the High

Street, which was literally just around the corner. Moments later he stopped the car in a side road and handed me a menu type list. He told me the film was mine to choose. Scanning the titles, there was one that jumped out at me. I'd heard one of my sisters talking to my Father about it a couple of weeks before, "That one," I said, "That is, if you don't mind?" I added, knowing my Parents wouldn't approve.

"Nope, that's fine. You wait here and I'll go and see if it's in," he said, leaving me alone in the car.

While I waited, an array or thoughts whizzed through my mind; what if I just got out? Just got out and ran? What if I kept running until I got to the safety of my house?

The idea alone settled my stomach, but only momentarily. What if he came looking for me? What if he caught up with me before I managed to get home?

And then there was school to consider. Even if I managed to get away today, it was only a matter of time before I would have to face him again.

Besides, he was trying to be nice. Perhaps he felt bad about that morning? I remember my thoughts bouncing from dark to light, and back again, until finally deciding that everything would turn out okay.

It would probably end up being a pleasant afternoon, if he didn't . . . and he wouldn't, not again; I was sure of it, sort of.

My train of thought was interrupted when Ropeman got back into the car. I cleared my throat in an attempt to rid myself of the bile slowly rising; the burning sensation was unfamiliar to me, but at least it was a distraction. It was too late now. And as the car

[37]

pulled away, pictures of his sofa and camera fixed in my mind. A copy of *The Texas Chainsaw Massacre* sat in his lap.

IN THE FLAT

As soon as I entered the lounge of the now all too familiar flat, I knew something bad was about to happen. My body felt like it was wrapped in invisible chains, and I smelt fear . . . my own fear. It was as though the atmosphere pulsated with such intensity that it grabbed me, shaking my flimsy little body, flaying my limbs in all directions, like some pathetic rag doll.

God, I was so terribly scared.

Ropeman left me alone while he went to the kitchen to sort out our drinks. The sight of the beer made me shudder, and the muscles that didn't tighten, twitched instead.

A dark and gloomy, musty smell,

A place no warmer than a prison cell,

Strange thoughts enter into your head,

You now start wishing you were tucked up in bed·

A frightening chill shoots through the air,

All you do is stand and stare,

It's a place with an eerie feeling,
Your heart by now is really speeding·
Sepulchre,
Sepulchre,
What a place,
Your heart is beating a rapid pace·
That awful chill is slowly rising,
All you think of is surviving,
But as you try to run and leave,
You can't help thinking your eyes deceive,
Lurking in that gloomy doorway,
Is something that's come out of doomsday,
You try to move, but are stuck to the spot,
You try to scream but breathing..., you're not·
Sepulchre,
Sepulchre,
What a place,
It's now your home·

To my relief, after handing me a beer, Ropeman slid the video cassette into the player, and we settled down to watch the film I was far too young to see. I tried to concentrate, but I was conscious of his every move; my muscles tightening at the slightest twitch.

It was an exceptionally good summer, so when

he asked if I was hot, I replied with a simple yes, pretending to be engrossed in the film. But I knew . . . in fact, every cell in my naïve young body sensed danger. And when he suggested I might be more comfortable if I removed my top, the fear enveloped me to the point of numbness, and before I knew it, there I was, stripped to the waist . . . again.

It wasn't long before the second stage of his sick plan was being put into action. "Shall we stretch out a bit? After all, there's plenty of room," he said. I felt like a rat caught in a trap, knowing there was no way out; no one was going to be knockin at the door and save me.

"Is it ok if I use the toilet?" I asked the question merely as an escape, something that would give me a bit more time, however limited it might be before the inevitable happened. Ropeman stopped the tape and directed me to the bathroom.

On returning to the lounge, I noticed that he'd removed his top. He was sprawled across the whole of the sofa, smiling, beckoning me to join him.

What choice did I have?

With a great deal of apprehension, which I'm convinced he was aware of, I did as I was asked. After awkwardly positioning myself into place, he began cuddling me from behind, pulling me closer before stroking my chest. Within seconds I felt his arousal in the small of my back. Without success I tried to ignore the feel of his sweaty fingers by losing myself in the movie.

Try as I might . . . and I did try, going so far as

to close my eyes and picturing myself saying the words, but somehow I couldn't summon the courage to tell him to stop.

My silence was deafening, and the sound of his erratic breathing all but consumed me, before I fell away.

You touched me,

Held me,

And stroked my chest,

Told me that you,

My teacher knew best·

I felt your hardness,

In the small of my back,

I had a chill in my spine,

When you said I'd be fine·

"I've always felt sorry for you, what with you being adopted and everything."

"It really is a pleasure to teach you"

"You've had a hard start to your life haven't you?"

"Try to relax a bit more, you feel so tense. I won't bite."

These were some of the things he was saying as he fondled me. I didn't respond. Instead, I closed my eyes and waited for the nightmare to end, ironically finding solace in the chaotic sounds blasting from the television.

After what seemed a lifetime, the movie finally came to an end. I eventually found the courage to say that I wanted to go home. To my astonishment my molester agreed, but he made me drink some strong coffee first.

An hour later I was in the safety of my bedroom, alone and isolated, but safe, unaware of the horrors that were waiting for me in the not too distant future.

Simon Palmer

BODY ARMOUR

As the start of the new school year loomed, the apprehension I felt about going back intensified to an astronomical level. Although my final year brought with it a new classroom and teacher, Ropeman would still be a prominent figure in my life for another ten months or so. He was always putting on film shows in the hall, and it was he who ran most of the music lessons which we were all expected to participate in. More often than not, he was the teacher allocated to take us along to the swimming baths once a week, and he was always the umpire when it came to a game of rounders.

It didn't take Ropeman long to approach me; in fact, it was only about an hour and a half into the first day back. He was on playground duty and I'd only been playing football for a few minutes before he pulled me to one side, asking me to come to his classroom at the end of the day. I was convinced that he wanted to arrange another "session" and the very thought of being touched again made my skin crawl, but there seemed to be absolutely no way out of the situation.

[45]

As the rest of the day progressed I realised the photo display had been shown. This gave me some hope that there would be no reason for him to suggest another "shoot" which eased my mind a little.

However, the worry of what it was he wanted tortured me for the rest of the day. And when the bell sounded, signifying that home time had arrived, my heart began pounding in my chest.

Opening the door, I walked in to find Ropeman sitting at his desk marking books. He offered me his usual sickly little smile and handed me a large brown envelope, "There you go young man, can you give this to your Mum for me?" Noticing the puzzlement on my face, he continued, "It's some of the photographs that I promised her."

"Oh, err, yeah."

"Can you tell her I said thank you? And if she ever wants any more taken, tell her to come see me." No, I thought to myself, as I pushed the memories of his touching me as far back into my mind as possible.

"Yeah I will. Can I go now.., I.., err, want to catch up with Peter?"

He leaned back in his chair, laughing, "Go on and scram."

Instead of making my way straight to Peter's house, I walked towards the local park to have a look at the pictures Ropeman had selected; surely they wouldn't be the "secret" ones he'd taken.

Sure enough, upon opening the envelope, I discovered it was only copies of the first few photos. Feeling happy my parents weren't going to discover anything, I ran home. It never occurred to me the

[46]

message for my Mum was going to result in yet more horrors for me to endure.

Riding my bike around the junior playground, I felt surprisingly relaxed as Ropeman stood in the centre taking snap shots. I'd gotten the bike as a combined birthday and Christmas present, and it was fantastic! Sporting three gears and drop handlebars, it was all that I was hoping for.

My Mother had spoken to Ropeman purely by chance after bumping into him outside the school, shortly after the Christmas break. He had somehow manipulated the conversation and re-suggested his offer of some more pics for the family album. With no reason to doubt the man's intentions, she decided to take him up on the offer, saying it would be nice to have some of me on the new bike.

Once again, it was a Saturday morning but because the whole scenario was taking place outside, I felt very much at ease, knowing he wouldn't dare try anything if there was a chance of his getting caught.

But apparently Ropeman was more determined than I could have predicted, and I walked into his trap yet again.

Part of the school buildings were very old, and made a strange contrast to the newest additions which had not long been erected. The playschool rooms were situated in what was once the main hall. It was a very big area with an extremely high ceiling, with the windows arched shaped and equally high. The bottom panes of glass were covered with various shades of transparent plastics, allowing the sun to cast an array of colours onto the reading carpet.

Somehow Ropeman had coaxed me into this area suggesting we take a few more photos "just for fun."

I expressed that maybe it was time for me to start making my way home, but even as the words fell from my mouth, I knew my passive protests were in vain. Less than ten minutes later, I found myself sitting in one of the small chairs with the camera clicking away, everything progressing in much the same way, until I was once again stripped to the waist.

And then, "just for fun," he asked if I fancied wearing just a triangle of material over my private area while sitting on the edge of one of the desks.

My head exploded like a volcano. I didn't know how to react, and found myself staring at the floor, counting the tiles surrounding my feet.

"If you don't want to it doesn't matter, I just thought it'd be a bit of a laugh."

Ropeman had given me a chance to walk away from his twisted offer, and until my time on this Earth is over, I will never understand why I declined it.

"It's not that I don't wanna do it."

"No one will find out if that's what you're concerned about. You won't get into any trouble or anything like that; we'd just keep it to ourselves, like we did the other stuff last year," he said, locking eyes with me without ever looking away.

"Okay then," I said, breaking his stare by focusing on the tiles again.

Losing the Hate

After my underpants were removed he positioned me on a tiny desk and pulled the smallest piece of white cloth from his pocket, clearly he had come prepared. As he began to carefully cover my privates with the flimsy material, I felt his fingers touch me. He apologised, but I could tell by the expression on his face and the sweat forming on his forehead, that he was by no means sorry.

Once happy with the pose, he gleefully stood back to take aim, like a hunter sizing up his prey. There is a belief held by some cultures that photographs can steal the spirit of a subject, and thinking back on it, with every click of his vile camera Ropeman had in effect chiseled away at mine, capturing my image forever, and leaving my spirit to bleed out for many years to come.

Again and again, the camera clicked as I tried to block all thoughts from my mind. After what seemed an eternity, he asked that I move my legs slightly further apart. The cloth fell from the precarious spot. Without warning and quick as a flash,he was there, "accidentally" touching me down below again.

Another dozen or so clicks of the shutter later, he quickly announced that we'd have to call it a day, saying I should put my clothes on straight away. It was as though he'd only just remembered an important appointment and couldn't wait to get me packed off home.

Sitting on a bench in the deserted swing park, clutching the screwed up ten pound note in my hands, tears began welling up in my eyes. Why was I being treated so badly by someone who was supposed to be looking out for me? And why was I so scared of telling the truth?

Convinced that I was to blame, an unexpected wave of anger exploded inside my body, an emotion so powerful I was unable to control it. And in a blind rage, I picked up my treasured new bike, throwing it as hard as my strength would allow against the railings around the swings. It didn't bother me that my parents had saved hard to buy it, and I didn't care that it would break their hearts when they found out what I had done. What did matter was that Ropeman had turned my perfect little world into a waking nightmare, and I had another ten pound note to prove it.

As the year progressed, I underwent a complete change of character. My relentless swearing began to push my Mum and Dad's sanity to its limits, and my schooling plummeted from about average to "could do better." Coupled with all of the bad language and my lack of drive to do well in my 11+, my parents were confronted with a heart breaking revelation; theft.

The rent tin was always kept in one of the kitchen cupboards, since no one in the family would have ever contemplated stealing; there was no reason for it to behidden. My pilfering began with the odd fifty pence, but when nothing was mentioned my greed made me braver and before long I was helping myself to larger and larger amounts. Inevitably, it led to a confrontation which ended with my storming out of the house, telling my Father to "fuck off!" as I went. I was eleven years old at the time.

Thinking it made me look big and tough, I started smoking, trying to impress my mates or anyone else who was around.

In fact, I was prepared to do anything, as long as it was against the rules.

Another of my habits was refusing to be home on time, and I'd often stay out until ten or eleven o'clock at night, showing total disregard for the discipline my parents tried to enforce.

None of the changes in my persona were in any way deliberate; I just began to change, each day becoming worse than the last. No matter how much I try to dissect what was happening, I cannot ever remember there being an in-between. It was as though one minute Simon Palmer was an average 11 year old kid, the next he'd transformed into a child from hell.

And so with my body armour flourishing around me, I walked out of school on the last day of term, knowing that I'd never enter the gates again. It was "hello" to my new school, and a fond farewell to that bastard Ropeman.

Simon Palmer

FINDING JOHNNY

The estate I lived on had nothing to offer in the way of activities, and playing football in the park had long since become a thing of the past. Most of my time was spent loitering on street corners, smoking with my friends and taking the piss out of whoever was unfortunate enough to be walking past.

It was on one of these evenings that I was introduced to something which would soon become an obsession, dominating my life for many years to come.

I was sitting on the wall that cordoned off a car park to some flats next to my house. My mate, Mark Milner, pulled a piece of paper out of the arse pocket of his tatty jeans, "Read this," he said, offering it to me.

"What is it?"

"Just fuckin' read it."

The paper contained lyrics to a song written by a rock group which had broken up with some fatal consequences after exploding into the charts a few years prior. As I began to read the words I found myself getting more and more excited, they were just amazing; exactly how I felt inside, words that I could

[53]

unequivocally relate to. They seemed to leap from the page and take hold of my heart, impregnating them inside of me. They were angry, goading, but most importantly, they made me realise that I was not the only angry person in the world.

So, with my clothes deliberately torn, and put back together with safety pins, and a head full of spikes, Simon Palmer became a clone of the most feared and hated man ever to explode into the lives of the general public; I became Johnny Rotten.

NEW BEGININGS (OLD FEARS)

Most of the other kids at my new school gave me a hard time because of the way I looked. I was forced by my year head to tone down the hairstyle and remove my earring, but the modified uniform I wore remained the same. And the earring and spikes did not remain gone for long. Months flew by with no reminders of the past except for the constant image of Ropeman still living in the darkest recesses of my mind. 11+ had removed the monster from my life; it was time to look to the future, to the fame and notoriety I'd become convinced was waiting for me.

      The only thing of any interest to me was music; there was no desire within me to become a bank manager or traffic warden, although being a traffic warden would have guaranteed the notoriety. My ambitions were focused purely on the music industry. It became impossible for me to stop writing, putting together basic verses and turning them into songs. My mind conjured images of stretch limo's, and television appearances, of a big house, and loads of money.

      Along with three others, a school band was formed. We called ourselves "Society's Rejects," each of us motivated by the same starry eyed fantasy.We were allowed to use the music room during the lunch break and it was during one of these sessions we gave birth to a song, an original song that I was proud to have written the lyrics to.

There's no future,
In this world for me,
Or can't you see.
I don't want you,
You don't want me,
I aint just a boy,
Or can't you see.
I'm living in fuckin' agony,
Tormented agony.
I'm living in fuckin' solitary.
I don't wanna,
I don't wanna be me,
I don't wanna,
Become a man,
I aint even happy as I am.
Are you so blind,
That you can't see,
As long as I live,
I won't ever be free.
I don't wanna,
I don't wanna be me.

I loved it, all four of us did. We asked if we could do a recording of the song being played, and to our complete astonishment, the music teacher said yes. She explained we'd have to speak to another teacher,

Mr. Caddy, who was in charge of all the school's electrical equipment, pretty much a similar role to the one Ropeman was involved in.

His room was based just off of the building's rear staircase on the first   floor. We went to see him straight away, finding it hard to refrain from running along the empty corridor. After rapping violently on the door, we all burst into the room. Without warning, my stomach lurched, before my head started spinning and I immediately felt physically sick.

It was like the instant just before an accident, when you know what's about to happen, but are powerless to stop it. I felt as if the world had paused momentarily, when my eyes focused on his. It was Ropeman, sitting casually next to Mr. Caddy, his now even chubbier face lit up at the sight of me. "Hello Simon, how's things?"

Chest pounding.

"I'm ok."

Smiling.

"Enjoying the new school?"

Fear rising.

"Yeah.., it's, it's alright."

Running.

"Sorry, sorry Mr. Caddy.., Sir, I need the toilet."

I left the room, and walked straight out of the school.

Simon Palmer

DREAMING, (WISHING)

How great it would be to fly. To soar up into the sky, higher and higher, not stopping until I reached a new world. A place where no one cried and where smiling was compulsory. Fields so full of bright and vibrant colours, it would be impossible to walk around without feeling a joy in your heart. A land where even the slightest of pain is nonexistent and vast rivers flow with crystal clear waters. Where a gentle breeze would weave its way through the branches of trees, making them sing so loud it was almost deafening, but pleasing at the same time.

Such a place might be called Heaven.
Of a love so great it was almost visible. A feeling of such intensity I felt a compulsion to reach out and grab hold of it, to savour it and keep it as mine forever. Perhaps it
would be possible for every soul inhabiting this special place to be linked together for all eternity, joined by

this wondrous power, smiling and laughing, and just being happy.

Suddenly, reality returned me to the park bench I was sitting on, just outside the school gates. A tear trickled down my cheek, would I ever be free of Ropeman? Was it my destiny to be stalked and tormented by him forever? My mind could not comprehend what he was doing at my new school, and I felt overwhelmed with paranoia, convinced he was only there because he knew I was. It felt as though he was telling me that things were not yet finished, and I felt so alone.

THINGS COME TO A HEAD

The following morning at registration I bounded through the classroom door ten minutes late, spoiling for some sort of confrontation. Mr. Brooke, my form tutor, looked straight at me, his face turning a deep shade of red, "You're late," he bellowed. I said nothing but fixed one of my stares on him, my eyes not blinking or looking anywhere other than directly into his.

He dismissed the class to their first lesson and told me to sit down. "What's going on Simon? Firstly, you walk out of school without so much as a bye or leave to anyone, and this morning you turn up late wearing a huge chip on your shoulder."

I said nothing.

It was apparent from the expression on Brooke's face that he could see something was troubling me, and it was manifesting itself in the form of bad behaviour. He sat down at his desk and spoke very softly, "C'mon, you're a bright lad with a tremendous amount going for you, what's it all about? Is there a problem at home?"

Here was my chance to speak out about Ropeman; he was giving me yet another green light to pour my heart out, but instead, I simply replied, "Bollocks."

Within seconds Brooke was upon me, and I was frog marched to the head master's office and with the adrenaline pumping through my veins, I prepared for battle.

(Inside the office)

HEADMASTER: Do you want to tell me what this is all about then sonny?

SIMON: There aint nothing' going on.

HEADMASTER: Simon, firstly you waltz out yesterday, secondly, after arriving late, obviously with issues on your mind, you swear at one of my staff. It really is unacceptable, now what's troubling you?

SIMON; FUCK OFF.

I gave the Head no choice but to suspend me; and for the second time in as many days I left school early. Lighting a cigarette, I headed down the road with a spring in my step. There would be no more chance meetings with Ropeman, not for a week at least. Flicking my fag butt away, I looked to the blue sky above me and breathed a sigh of relief. I wanted to be alone, away from the adult world of manipulation and complexities; I wanted to be a child again.

[62]

A STATE OF EUPHORIA

My school suspension was lifted exactly one week later and things carried on much the same as usual. I continued to be the mixed up problem child who no one had any time for (except for the love that my family continued to offer), swearing and cursing my way through life. When my form tutor told me the lunchtime music practice had been revoked, I saw a green light for truancy.

Accompanied by the drummer of my band, Sean Watson, most of our days were spent reeking havoc on the infamous Ferrier estate in Kidbrooke. When tired of throwing stones at people's windows, we'd steal large quantities of milk off the milkman and hide ourselves high up on the balconies, pouring it on unsuspecting passers by as they walked through the many rabbit warren type pathways. We would often collapse in uncontrollable fits of hysteria as our victims tried in vain to apprehend us.

One particular afternoon saw us both have a crack at shoplifting, our target being a local hardware store, hoping if nothing else, we'd get chased by the manager.

Sean created a distraction by talking to the man about a Saturday job, while I committed the actual theft.

I grabbed the first thing that my trembling hand rested on and slipped the object into my blazer before silently walking out of the shop to the freedom that eagerly awaited me. I was about to cross the road when the sound of heavy footfalls boomed behind me. Spinning on my heels, I expected to come face to face with an irate shop manager, but to my relief it was Sean, "What is it? What did ya nick?"

"Fuck knows." I put my hand into my pocket and pulled the mystery object out; it was a large tube of Evostick.

A short time later we were crawling through the tiniest of gaps behind a low level car park, and totally oblivious to the world that surrounded us; we introduced ourselves to the fine art of glue sniffing.
I cannot speak for Sean, but for me it was the most awesome thing I'd ever done. It completely transformed the way I thought; there was no pain or fear, and I felt no sadness whatsoever. The make believe world I had so often dreamt about began to flourish, enfolding me within all its glory.

Crisp blue skies,

A sun so bright,

Losing the Hate

Sweet smelling flowers,
Birds taking flight·
An ocean of colour,
The horizon so bright,
A feeling of hope,
And nothing to fear·
Beautiful hills,
And fields full of corn
Chairs in the garden,
Swings on the lawn·
The howling of wolves,
Death and decay,
A dread in the heart,
At the start of the day·
Scared of the shadows,
And what they contain,
Contorted illusions,
Of a brain that's insane·

    I began to sniff glue on a regular basis; enthralled by the way it made me feel. Every opportunity I got was spent with a carrier bag at my mouth, escaping the hell that had become my world.

    During the periods when I wasn't high, and the way the come down left me feeling, a new kind of anger started to emerge, giving me a compulsion to inflict harm on myself, as well as becoming more physically violent towards others.

I soon started picking on the locals, demanding that they give me their pocket money, threatening to beat them up if they told their parents, (and sometimes beating them up anyway). Every time a cat or dog came near me, I would lash out as hard as my strength would allow.

At times they appeared to have his grotesque smile, and this could send me over the edge. Sometimes I'd sit for hours within the confines of my room, stabbing my arm with a sewing needle. I'd stab harder and harder, enjoyingthe burning pain it caused. It took my mind off the memories, images which now tormented my brain on a daily basis, except for the occasions when the glue took me away.

PART TWO:
A DIFFERENT KIND OF TERROR

Simon Palmer

A NEW DISEASE (EARLY 1982)

Over the following year, my behaviour steadily worsened (if that was at all possible). My parents would say one thing and I'd go out of my way to create as much bad feeling as I possibly could by doing the complete opposite. I wanted to make everyone else pay for the way I was feeling inside, no matter what it cost me. My stomach felt as though it had been wrenched from my body with a butcher's knife, like it was trailing behind me wherever I went. The pain throbbing inside my skull was getting close to some sort of explosion and it felt like there was nothing that I could do to stop it.

And then it came……

Something to push me over the edge……

For the past month or so I'd been trying to wear my parents down by constantly whining, telling them my ways would change if they bought me a C.B radio. All of my mates had one perched nicely beside their beds, and I aimed to get one too, by any means possible. From what I can remember, a basic model was around £100 and after several rows with Mum and Dad, I eventually got my own way.

And then it came……

Something to push me over the edge……..

Instead of making a whole new world of friends, I was confronted with two of the most evil creatures ever to walk on God's Earth.

STRAIGHT FROM THE HEART

So far I've found this extremely hard emotionally. As well as reliving my ordeal, I've also been remembering certain episodes which are yet to come. Pictures have been popping into my head at random, in no particular order whatsoever. It's a part of my life I never dreamed would be purposely re- visited, but I am truly pleased by my decision to do so.

Due to the nature of what you're about to read in, I have opted to write in "head speak." My mind is awash with images and conversations, all of which entwine together with no beginning or end, and for that reason, I would like to write this section exactly as it appears to me.

I think, in all honesty, if I don't write it straight from the head, directly as it comes, then it may not ever find its end, which is something I need to reach . . . the end. For maybe then I'll be able to move on, in search of the happiness I desperately crave.

Simon Palmer

BREAKER ONE-FOUR

I can't altogether clearly remember how I came to meet up with Flower Queen and Secret Squirrel, or when the first introductions took place for that matter.

I do recall speaking to them over the CB on a fairly regular basis and together with my mate Peter, began to visit their house on quite a number of occasions, generally having a bit 0f a laugh and sponging cigarettes.

Both Flower Queen and Secret Squirrel, (who will be known as Karen and Stuart), would often invite people from the CB radio to their house for an "eyeball," (slang for meet), and I'm pretty sure that's how I first came to go there myself.

Karen was in her mid forties, with long flowing black hair. She stood about 5'4" (ish) and dressed more like she was in her early twenties. Stuart on the other hand was closer to his mid fifties and looked as though he'd had a real rough upbringing, a collage of home-made tattoos spread across both arms, his face covered with a mixture of wrinkles and scars.

[73]

Peter and I had gone to their house and the only place for me to sit was on a small footstall close to the open fire which dominated the room. It was a full house, with many people I'd never met before and the cigarettes were being passed around like sweets in a playground.

I remember we had to suffer cups of tea made with sterilised milk. One by one, as the time ticked by, people made their pleasantries and left. Before long it was just Peter and I who were still eager for idle chat. For some reason every time I tried to move from the foot stool to an empty seat, Stuart told me to stay where I was. Apart from seeming a little strange, I thought nothing more of it.

Karen, who was sitting directly opposite me on the sofa, said that my image would look a lot better if my hair was bleached blond. I explained my pocket money wouldn't stretch for a visit to the hairdressers, when Stuart piped up, "Karen'll do it for ya. She used to do mine."

She nodded in agreement and before long I was making arrangements to go back around . . . alone.

Peter and I announced our intention to leave, and when we stood, I noticed Stuart giving me a strange sort of smile.

The next time I saw them was a few days later. I'd been to the chemist, bought some hair dye, and headed out for my transformation.

Sitting on the sofa, and with Karen busy making a pot of tea in the kitchen, Stuart began talking to me in a way that left me feeling frightened and embarrassed.

He told me he'd noticed my looking up Karen's skirt the last time I was there. I told him I wasn't doing anything of the sort and he just laughed, "I really don't blame you looking," he said, "After all, she's horny as hell aint she?"

Before I had a chance to answer the lounge door opened, there stood Karen. I could feel myself shaking and all of the recent past with Ropeman came flooding back. The fear I'd felt was suddenly very fresh in my young mind. Karen poured me a cuppa and told Stu to stop trying to embarrass me.

And then it started.

Karen sat beside me and offered a cigarette. When I reached for it, Stu told her not to give it to me, unless she had a "feel" first. It was all done in a very humorous way, but that didn't stop my fear from mounting. The same sickly feelings were resurfacing. I wanted to tell them both to fuck off, run from their house and tell my parents everything, but I didn't.

Instead I played along with the joke. Before I knew what was happening Karen's hand was between my legs, she was squeezing me. I noticed Stu watching and realised he'd started to rub himself, and his grin made me shudder. It was the same disgusting expression I was trying so hard to forget; it was like seeing Ropeman's grin plastered on Stuart's face.

Karen finally removed her hand and gave me the cigarette. My nerves calmed a little, thinking the "joke" was over, when quick as a flash, Stu was kneeling between my legs. He asked me if I wanted to f**k Karen.

I said nothing.

[75]

Simon Palmer

Stuart then explained that Karen had been told by the doctor it was only a matter of a year or so before she'd be confined to a wheelchair, due to an arthritic spine. He claimed the Dr. suggested she be allowed to "enjoy herself" as much as possible before that time came.

He tugged at my wrist, encouraging me to the floor, and then forced Karen's legs open, telling me to have a look, "Wouldn't you just love to shove your d*** up there right now?"

I didn't answer.

Karen was telling him to stop, but she was giggling as she said it, claiming to be embarrassed.

Stu didn't force me to have sex with Karen that day, but it ended with me putting myself away after he'd taken my young manhood into his mouth in an attempt to arouse me.

An hour later I was having my hair washed. Once the peroxide was rinsed away, and I'd wiped the surplus water from my eyes, Karen asked me for a kiss to say thank you. Before I could respond her mouth was connecting with mine.

I followed her back into the lounge feeling a bit disorientated. Stu immediately asked if she'd managed to scrounge a kiss. The smile on her face embarrassed me, but it answered his question. I wanted to leave, but I thought it rude, since Karen had just finished with my hair. I fidgeted, the knot in my stomach making it difficult to sit still. Before long, Stu had managed to shift the conversation; the subject naturally centred on sex. He asked me if I'd had a w**k before coming to their house. When I told him I hadn't, he questioned me as to why I never got aroused earlier. Because you're a disgusting man and I'm a kid was what I felt like shouting, but I didn't answer.

Eventually, when I announced it was time for me to go home for tea, Karen asked if I'd be popping around to see them the next day. And once again, for reasons I don't understand to this day . . . I said yes.

Simon Palmer

THE SECOND VISIT

I hadn't made any arrangements for the following day, and as I took the short walk from my front door to Stuart and Karen's house, the apprehension that swept over me was almost suffocating, as was the fear that violently churned in the pit of my stomach.

Sleep had, surprisingly, greeted me fairly quickly the night before; my mind had not yet fully digested what had happened. But as I neared the destination, inching my way forward, my head became awash with the frightening details of the encounters I'd had over the last couple of years.

The photo sessions with Ropeman, the sexual contact Stu had subjected me to; I began to wonder if it was all part and parcel of normal adult life. But mostly, I was scared of them. Afraid that if I didn't show up, one of them would say something to my parents about what had taken place. And truth be told, I was terrified. Stu frightened me more than anyone I'd ever met.

Karen opened the door and gave me a warm smile. It wasn't the sickly smile of Ropeman, nor was it the twisted grin I'd seen on Stu's face the previous day, but I still felt an almost irrepressible urge to smack the smile clean off her face. She was evil; not nearly as intimidating as Stu, but evil just the same.

I walked past her and strutted into the lounge, my blond spikes erupting from my skull in all their glory. "Alright Stu." he looked up from his paper, his bright blue eyes seemed to sparkle, and for the first time I noticed just how scarred his face actually was.

Karen came up behind me, I felt her hand on my shoulder, and "Don't I get a kiss then"?

I didn't know where to look, much less what to say. I'm not sure if it was visible, but my whole body felt as though it was physically shaking. I tried to make a joke of it and simply kissed her on the cheek, quickly rubbing my lips with the back of my hand and pretending to be sick, mimicking the actions of a four or five year old child.

After sitting on the sofa, I asked Stuart if it was okay to turn on the CB, which was on a small table between where I was sitting and his armchair. "Leave it off for the minute," he replied, "maybe we'll put it on after a cuppa."

Before I could do or say anything else he told me to stand in front of him, telling me I was wearing my studded belt all wrong. I did as was asked, and he began rubbing my crutch.

Like the day before, he asked if I'd had a w**k before coming round. I nodded, hoping it would keep things from going further, but it just made him all the more eager to try and get me aroused. Karen, who was once again standing behind me, placed her hand on my bum. Within seconds her hand had moved down and was easing my legs apart from behind, moving ever closer to my testicles. Before I knew what was happening, Stu was massaging my penis with both hands.

"Surely you must be able to get a h**d on with a gorgeous woman like that standing behind you?"

He looked up at me with that all too familiar sickly smile I'd become so accustomed to, before shifting me around to face Karen. It was now her turn. The fear inside me was worse than ever, and I honestly thought I was going to die; my heart beating so fast I expected it to explode at any minute.

Stuart stood up and started to push himself into my rear and I immediately felt his arousal. He instructed Karen to take me to the sofa, as he made his way over to the table by the bay windows.

"You two enjoy yourselves, an' I'll sit here, make sure no one looks in or anything." He was still rubbing himself.

Karen sat on the sofa, parted her legs, and told me to kneel in front of her. And as repulsive as the idea was, my body betrayed me, and I became aroused.

After hitching her skirt up, she gave me instructions . . . but I couldn't, instead I just knelt there, absolutely frozen. I guess Stuart was becoming impatient; he began making a joke of things as was his way, and came up behind me. He gave me a gentle shove in the hopes of my finding the unwanted destination eagerly awaiting me.

Eventually, the goal was indeed found.

I was thirteen by this time.

Once I had satisfied her, and the ordeal was over, Stuart abruptly told Karen to take me in the bathroom and give me a "wash", saying that it was "important to keep clean."

Looking back, I fully understand the real reason for this. It was done to wash away the physical evidence.

After making sure I was thoroughly "clean," Karen pushed me against the bathroom wall, and stared into my eyes, "Don't lead me on will you. If you want it to stop don't go and start seeing someone else behind my back, just tell me first," she said, as if we were a couple of love struck teenagers, her eyes seemed to be lost in mine.

All I wanted at that moment was to get away from her, from them . . . but I was too scared to say so. I was so confused, so utterly befuddled. Why was this happening to me? Why couldn't I just tell them to fuck off, and be done with it?

The sight of Stuart smiling once we made our way back into the front room only served to humiliate me further.

I truly wanted my life to end.

ONGOING EVENTS

After that incident, I should have run, hit the pavement and screamed from the rooftops. I should have told anyone willing to listen what they had done to me. Most especially my parents, I should have gone to them, but I couldn't help thinking that if no one believed me, it would only make things worse. I'd inevitably have to disclose the past events with Ropeman, and coupled with the way I'd been behaving over the last few years, I was sure I'd be looked upon as a fantasist; just another lie from the strange mind of Simon Palmer.

What's worse, I was utterly convinced if I continued to keep my silence, and refrained from going back to Stu and Karen's, they would almost certainly come looking, and that thought terrified me most of all.

Apart from keeping all this to myself, I was confronted with another dilemma. What was I supposed to tell my friends? They were used to my being around and to suddenly disappear without a trace, how was I supposed to deal with that?

Confusion was rapidly seeping into my world; and combined with the fear which was paramount within me; my behaviour at home fell to an all time low, school remaining a complete non event. The truancy became so much of an issue that the authorities assigned me a social worker, who in turn, suggested my parents agree to me seeing a child psychologist.

Numerous opportunities to tell the official bodies presented themselves, but I steadfastly remained silent. The lies continued, and so did the abuse.

Peter Simpson, along with Mark Milner, two of the greatest friends anyone could have asked for, began to see less and less of me. On the rare occasion when I did see them, it felt like something had changed, like our friendship was over; we no longer had anything in common, or so it seemed.

Besides I didn't have time for them anymore, not really; Stu and Karen had taken over my life; and as soon as the day's truancy was completed I headed straight for their house, but I truly missed hanging out with my mates.

I remember an occasion when Peter and I cycled to Mark's, getting completely drenched in a heavy downpour of rain. As always, upon arriving, his Mother Doreen, welcomed us as if we were her own, slaving over a stove to cook a piping hot meal. Not because she felt obliged to, it was just the way things had always been between us. There were many other occasions when I'd bound into the kitchen and tell my Mum that Mark was staying for Sunday lunch, "Ok, but if he don't wash his hands he'll be eating bread an' drippin'," she'd say. Mark and Peter were almost family, and I missed them with all my heart, but mostly I missed being a boy.

As the weeks turned to months, my daily visits became nothing more than routine, as did the abuse, which was happening on an equally regular basis.

Stuart had gradually become physically more and more involved, and even made some security measures; doctoring the front gate so we'd hear their Son Julian if he happened to arrive home earlier than expected.

It was not uncommon for Stuart to be the one to start the touching and kissing, and when it came to other "oral activities" he was always more than eager to get the ball rolling, often leaving Karen on the sidelines to watch.

I remember the suppressed anger bubbling away inside me, the same anger which dwells within me today, like a wild animal tearing at the ground beneath the bars of a cage, desperately trying to free itself from the boundaries of confinement.

It was a totally different and more intense form of abuse, far removed from the scenarios Ropeman subjected me to. I felt deeply afraid of Stuart and what he might do if I were to refuse them. As well as being a monster, Stu was clever, and he was by all accounts a master manipulator. I'd often been told stories of how he'd beaten, even killed people while allegedly serving in the army. And from the looks of him, it was easy to picture him doing it. Sometimes I even imagined him beating me to a bloody pulp.

It was clear he had no conscience, and I was only as safe as I was useful. As long as I continued to perform, all was well. After all, Simon was Stuart's favourite plaything, a toy, one with a very specific purpose.

One evening, in the early part of 1983, I was struck with a sudden wave of bravery. On impulse, I decided against showing up at their house, instead walking about two or three miles in no particular direction. It was exhilarating; I hadn't had any "Simon time," for ages. For those fleeting hours, I had my freedom back. It even felt as though my mind was becoming clearer, the confusion lifting temporarily as I bumbled about aimlessly. And to some degree, there was a certain amount of pride simmering below the surface of my newly found sense of well-being.

I was at last standing up to him, up to them. And boy was I going to regret it.

It must have been at least eleven o'clock as I rounded the corner and heard my name being called. Half expecting to see my Father, I turned, my stomach dropped. My worst fears were now confirmed, they were standing in the shadows, just out of view from my house. Although I had always suspected they would come for me, I was taken off guard by how brash they were about it. In front of my home, my family just yards away, there they were, both of their faces filled with so much rage, I honestly thought that I was about to get a bloody good hiding.

"Where've you been then?"

Without thinking, I lied, telling them my cousin had just dropped me off down the road, explaining he'd come over earlier and taken me for a spin in his car.

Stuart was having none of it; he was convinced I'd been with a girl and that I was taking the piss out of him.

Desperate not to be discovered by any family members, and scared of being beaten to death, I told them I needed to get indoors, otherwise my father would soon be looking for me, adding that I'd come around straight after school (truanting). Stuart shot me a look, one that indicated I better be there . . . or else.

I gave him my word, promising faithfully to come around, before I stammered away, my legs wobbly and weak from the confrontation.

At a quarter to four the following day I was absolutely terrified, to the point of nausea, sure I was going to be sick at any moment. The front door opened before my hand even managed to reach for the brass door knocker. Karen was standing in front of me, "You made it then. Come on, in you come."

Country and western music was playing and I could hear Stuart trying his best to sing along, and failing miserably. Walking as slowly as I possible could, I entered the lounge. To my surprise the greeting was by no means what I'd expected. A can of lager was shoved into my hand and Karen told me to help myself to a fag. Far from the bollocking I was expecting, they were treating me as if it were my birthday, and I thought the evening might turn out okay for a change.

After some heavy drinking, Stuart asked me why I'd chosen to stay away the night before, "I can't believe you'd rather spend the night with yer cousinthan to be cocking Karen."

He gestured me over, "Let's see if I can't get yer going."

Yet again I found myself standing in front of his armchair, not knowing where to look as he rubbed my penis through the fabric of my jeans. Karen was sprawled on the sofa, her legs apart and touching herself; looking at me as she did so.

After what seemed like hours, I was told to sit at the table and "get myself out". Stu was kneeling on the floor in front of Karen by this time and they had sex right there in front of me.

I was fourteen years old.

When they'd finished I was ordered, literally, to give Karen oral satisfaction, and Stuart got on his knees beside me, aiming a torch between her legs, making sure it was done properly.

BACK TO SCHOOL

Following a court case at Camberwell Juvenile Court for truanting, the judge informed me, along with my parents, that if I persisted with my refusal to attend school, then he'd have no hesitation in placing me in an assessment centre, at which time my fate would be decided. He added that a boarding school would not be ruled out of the equation.

My parents were far from happy; apart from the fact their daughters were not nearly the burden I was proving to be. Neither of them had ever been inside a court room in their lives, and I had brought shame and embarrassment crashing down on their shoulders, as well as my own.

In fact, they'd gone so far as to pay a visit to Stuart and Karen, hoping they could throw some light on why I was behaving in such an unacceptable manner. My parents were under the impression my afternoon visits were with Julian, Stuart and Karen's son. They were attempting to reach out to fellow parents for help, desperate to figure out the cause of my behaviour. If only they knew, but they didn't . . . I made very sure of that.

[89]

Being as frightened of going "away," as disclosing my secrets, I reluctantly began to attend school. It wasn't too bad settling back into the mundane regime of the education system, but although I was in attendance every day, it didn't stop me from being as disruptive as ever. Due to the disruption I was causing, and coupled with the amount of learning I'd missed out on, a lot of the teachers were reluctant to have me included within the class. A relatively new member of the teaching team was a man called Mr. Jenkins; he ran the remedial classes, which is where I was sent during the periods of exclusion from some of my lessons.

In the beginning my attitude towards Jenkins was no different to any of the other teachers, but that soon changed. He was an exceptionally good man, who treated me like a human being, and I respected him, my admiration growing as the time we spent together increased. We'd sit and debate almost everything; he'd try to warn me about the complexities of life, things which I would inevitably have to face. But he was not condescending about it, asking for my opinions, rather than telling me his. In effect, Mr. Jenkins treated me as an equal.

I'm not sure what the man saw in me, but I'm certain he didn't see me as the rogue others portrayed me to be. I was born of my circumstances; forces beynd my control had created me.

He was one of the few people who could see through my armour, and it was nice to view myself through his eyes. And for this reason alone, whenever I think back to my brief times in his presence, I have nothing but admiration for him.

[90]

A TRIP TO THE SEASIDE

I was desperate to get a tattoo, it became an obsession, but even creatures like Stuart and Karen were not very forthcoming in helping me achieve this goal.

It occurred to me, there was another creature in my life, one I hadn't seen in some time, and I didn't relish seeing him again, not by any means, but I was determined, and as far as I was concerned, he owed me.

I instinctively knew if I hung around long enough it would only be a matter of time before I came face to face with the man who had already played a big part in fucking my life up.

And just as expected, it only took twenty minutes of patience before I spied the chubby prick walking towards his car.

"Hello Sir," I called. The sickly smile I was accustomed to Stuart wearing now, suddenly returned to the face of its original master.

"Hello stranger, how the devil are you?" he seemed genuinely pleased to see me.

"Yeah, I'm cool ta."

"Haven't seen you for ages, how's it all going?" he asked.

I dangled the carrot.

"School's shit, they stopped the band 'cause of me makin' trouble all the time."

A look of dissatisfaction replaced his grin, but before he had a chance to comment, I continued my campaign on behalf of the body art I so desperately craved.

"I, I was err, wondering if you wanted to do some more photos?"

SELLING MY SOUL

The last thing I had expected was to put myself in yet another precarious position. But I wasn't a young lad anymore, I was now close to Ropeman in size, and he was far too physically unfit to actually threaten me.

Besides, in my mind, I was a thug, a real tough guy, so I hadn't counted on reverting back to being a ten year old in his presence, but that's exactly what happened. Insecurities flooded my mind as the memories mercilessly taunted me. It was almost impossible for me to look at the man's face; but the die had been cast.

And for some reason, I couldn't bring myself to call it off. It seems incomprehensible now, but I still wanted that damn tattoo, eventually selling my soul to the devil to get it.

The events resulting from my actions that day are among my most difficult memories to deal with. In large part because it was my own doing, I have no xcuses, and I couldn't offer up an explanation if I tried.

[93]

I instigated it, and that shame will follow me to the grave.

There are times when my heart is riddled with hatred and utter contempt, when I want to strike out and get my revenge. I crave that retribution, and pity myself for the lack thereof. But there have also been many dark, very drunken nights when I detest the face staring back at me from the mirror, knowing, that at least in my view, the reflection is not completely innocent.

THE MOUSETRAP

The look on Ropeman's face was one of utter surprise, but I could see he was eager to take me up on my offer, and so I jumped straight in with my request, "I don't s'pose you know where I might be able to get a tattoo done do ya?"

"Nah, wouldn't have foggiest," his response was immediate. Knowing he was suspicious, I shrugged and turned to walk away.

"Wait!"

I hesitated before facing him again, already thinking better of my proposal. My jaws tensed, and it took a conscious effort to keep from clenching my fists. Maybe it was the slightly frantic tone in his voice, I was reacting to?

He was sick a bastard.

"Yeah?"

"Meet me outside the swimming baths."

He must have picked up on my hesitance, I was having second thoughts.

"I'll make some inquiries," he said, his turn to dangle the carrot.

[95]

After making the arrangements, I set out for my usual appointment.

When I arrived, Karen was alone. My encounter with Ropeman still fresh in mind, this was the last thing I needed.

As afraid as I was of Stuart, the thought of being alone with her made me shudder, literally. Although thankfully, our being together without Stuart around was a rare occurrence, but her demeanour changed dramatically when it did happen. It was as if she thought of me as her lover, as if I were deriving just as much pleasure from the arrangement.

Sometimes I wondered if she realized that from my perspective it was a chore, a repulsive one at that. There was nothing about her I felt attracted to. I just did what I was told, functioning like a machine, somehow detaching myself from reality; completely unaware that their perversions would pollute the very essence of my being. She was my capture, and if I felt anything for her at all, it certainly wasn't love.

"Stuart wants us to meet him at the park," she announced, her face bitter with resentment, but it was music to my ears. I would have been happy if she were delivering me to the devil himself, anything was better than being stuck alone in the house with her.

As we made our way towards the park where Stuart gardened, I casually mentioned it would be difficult for me to visit on Sunday, claiming relatives were invited for dinner. She wasn't pleased by any means, but agreed to square it with Stu.

[96]

The rest of the way I spoke mainly about what it was going to be like when I became a famous punk star. Anyone passing by would never have guessed that Karen was party to sexually abusing me. I could have easily been her son.

She kept her word, and Stuart agreed to give me the day off. Ironically, I was actually looking forward to seeing Ropeman. My encounters with Stuart and Karen were becoming increasingly depraved, and I'd recently began to wonder if Stuart sensed that his wife's interest in me wasn't purely sexual.

Given the complexities at play in my young life, I reasoned Ropeman wasn't much of threat after all. Another photo shoot was the least of my concerns.

"Alright fella?" he asked as I slid into the front seat and fastened my safety belt. His smile seemed almost natural, as if he was genuinely pleased to see me.

As we headed towards the High Street, Ropeman mentioned he'd found a studio that might be willing to do the work on me, but it was in Southend on Sea. I told him time wasn't a problem; it didn't matter how far away it was.

And so the journey began.

I was still in very young and impressionable stage of life, probably more so due to the abuse. It was, looking back; extremely naïve of me to believe there would be anyone stupid enough to put their livelihood on the line by tattooing a minor. But I did believe it and Ropeman knew that.

[97]

An awful lot of the outward journey is locked away, and try as I might, I cannot recall what the two of us spoke about. I'm assuming it's locked away due to its total insignificance, devoured by the haunting memories of the homeward bound drive.

As the car came to a halt on the seafront, Ropeman thrust a ten pound note into my hand, telling me the three pounds I'd brought was by no means enough.

It was planned, once I'd finished at the studio, I was to hang around the entrance to the pier. This is where Ropeman would catch up with me.

My adrenaline pumping I made my way along the esplanade, visions of body art fuelling my excitement. After climbing a few steps, my hand grasped the door handle and I thrust myself into the unknown, expecting to be confronted by a motley crew of heavily tattooed biker types.

But the shop was empty.

Seeing another doorway at the far end of the shop, I pigeon stepped towards it, stopping briefly to look at the pictures adorning the walls of what appeared to be a waiting room. I was suddenly startled by a menacing looking man sporting a ZZ Top style beard. It was apparent from the expression on the guy's face that my wishful thinking was in no way going to be honoured. I didn't even bother asking, lying instead by claiming my brother had sent me down with a price enquiry.

"How much for a small eagle?" I asked to make my claim appear legitimate.

"Bout twenty five quid," he said, his stare unwavering as I sheepishly tried to keep my eyes locked to his.

Spinning on my heels, I exited the shop as quickly as my legs would carry me, fearing the man would surely eat me alive at any moment.

It was only a matter of minutes before I found myself waiting for Ropeman to appear at the designated spot, and as if by some strange form of magic, he seemed to pop up from nowhere.

"How'd you get on?" he enquired.

Keeping the truth to myself, I claimed that a biker bloke told me I was too young and threw me out. It was clear by the look on Ropeman's face he was fully expecting me to say something along those lines.

"Tell you what Si, how'd you fancy taking a look at the fairground? We may as well make the journey a bit more worthwhile for you."

I jumped at the suggestion, a fresh wave of adrenaline coursing through my veins, "Yeah, cool!"

We silently walked along the promenade and all manner of questions were flitting around inside my head. How could this man have possibly meant to cause me so much pain? Why did I fear him so much? Perhaps what he's said and done to me was just his way of being nice. Maybe it was just the way adults did things? After all, Stuart and Karen were doing far worse than this man had ever done. I was so lost within my thoughts it took Ropeman several attempts to bring me back to Earth. "Simon. Si', are you alright?"

"Oh, err, yeah. Sorry, I was miles away."

[99]

Once inside the amusement park I made a bee line for the Mouse Trap, a rickety old rollercoaster, and I'm sure Ropeman had to break into a trot to keep up with me.

Anyone who happened to pay us even the slightest of a sideways glance would have surely thought we were Father and Son, enjoying a grand day out.

Ropeman sat behind me in the brightly coloured car made to look like a mouse.

He laughed.

And I screamed, having more fun than I'd had in ages.

The pain this man had caused me, the pain which was presently being intensified by Stuart and Karen was for the moment gone. I was happy, genuinely thrilled to be alive.

And I liked him.

He'd turned out to be a good man after all, not the monster I once imagined him to be.

He was indeed a good man, wasn't he?

MY WORLD CAME TUMBLING DOWN
(AGAIN)

For a fleeting moment I felt alive, and strangely hopeful, somehow managing to surface from the murky abyss I had come to know as my existence. The sensation of feeling carefree was foreign to me; in fact, feeling any emotion was a rarity. With exception to the rage which seemed to be an almost constant companion, as much a part of me now as my own shadow.

Ropeman had not even mentioned the photo shot, which only added to my euphoric stupor. But letting down my guard always had its consequences, and as it turned out, this day would not prove to be an exception.

Feeling at ease, and having somehow bonded with my molester, I thought about breaking my silence. The situation with Stuart and Karen was unbearable. It was an absolute nightmare; I was filled with shame and ready to reach out for help. Why I would choose this man to confide in is beyond me, but I suppose it's just another example of what a truly damaged young man I was.

Being naïve I actually believed he could be of help. After all, he was a teacher, a well respected member of the community. He could certainly give me some guidance in the matter?

I didn't get a chance to voice my misguided plea for help. Once again, he tore my world apart, pushing me even closer to the end of my tether when he began bombarding me with questions; inquiries which not only made me uncomfortable, but embarrassed me terribly.

"Have you got a girlfriend yet?" he asked.

"Yeah," I lied.

"What's her name?"

Already expecting him to ask, I blurted a made up name, "Debbie . . . Debbie Kent."

"Have you had her yet?" I didn't know what he meant and told him so.

"Has she let you fuck her yet?" The fear suddenly erupted, exploding from the top of my head. I couldn't even put the words together to respond.

"She must have let you touch her?"

"Yeah . . . yeah course she has!" The silence in the car was deafening. I could hear nothing but my heart beat.

"Have you seen inside her knickers?"

In hindsight, it's clear he was probing my sexual awareness, trying to get a gage on how sexually experienced I had become; but my youth combined with a complete lack of understanding blinded me from recognizing the manipulation for what it was.

The subject of my imaginary girlfriend was dropped, and the rest of the trip back to London was one of few words. Focusing all my attention on passing images, I tried to ignore his presence, only honouring him with an occasional one word response.

Once the car came to a halt a few hundred yards from my front door, I relaxed, somewhat, but there was something on his mind, so letting down my guard was out of the question.

"Here we are then, back all safe and sound," he said, the tone of his voice artificially kind.

"Cheers for takin' me."

"The pleasure was all mine, I'm only sorry it didn't turn out better for you."

I unclipped my safety belt and tried hard not to look at him, "Don't matter, s'pose I'll get one done somewhere else."

Ropeman was shifting in his seat, tapping a tuneless rhythm on the steering wheel.

Before I could make an escape, he said, "Listen, before you go, did you; I mean was you serious the other day?"

Now it was my turn to shift uncomfortably, "what about? D'you mean the tattoo?"

I tried to play dumb, knowing full-well what was coming next, or at least that's what I thought.

"No, no I know you want one, no I . . . I meant about doing some more pics?"

Before I had a chance to answer he hit me with both barrels.

"I know this bloke who, well he publishes photographs in a magazine, and I, well, I just wondered if you fancied making a bit of extra cash?"

[103]

"What, what sort of photos? You mean like last time?"

"Well, yeah, sort of. We'd probably have to jazz them up a bit. I could get you about twenty quid a time out of it."

"Yeah, alright then," I answered, ignoring the "cat that got the cream," expression crossing over his flushed face.

"Ok, if you're sure?"

I nodded, and made a clumsy exit from the confined space.

We arranged for me to wag off school the following Tuesday.

A VERY DIFFERENT PHOTO SHOOT

We met outside Ladywell railway station at nine-thirty in the morning, our destination, a beautiful house in the up market part of Catford. As we entered the lounge my jaw dropped in awe. It was gigantic! The pale green walls, showcasing an elegant three piece leather suite, everything was perfectly arranged. An enormous television positioned by the sparkling bay window dominated the room.

Ropeman informed me he'd taken the liberty of borrowing some "special garments." He smiled, assuring me they were perfect for the style of pictures he planned on taking. A wave of apprehension swept over me when he handed me the carrier bag on his way out of the room.

"Why don't you try something on? I'll sort out some coffee," he yelled from behind closed doors.
"What have I done?" I thought to myself, sifting through the bag, the safety of my room appearing in my

mind's eye, along with an overwhelming craving for my treasured glue.

"Oh God, I can't do this," I muttered, my tongue adhering itself unnaturally to the roof of my mouth. When the sound of the heavy footsteps warned of his impending return, my body began to shake uncontrollably.

"Everything okay fella?" The bastard asked with feigned concern. Clearly, I was not "okay," the intensity with which my hand vibrated as I accepted the coffee should have told him that. But he only had one concern and my well being was hardly an issue.

"How about I leave the room while you get changed? Give me a shout when you're ready," he said rather sternly, before looking over his shoulder directly into my eyes to reiterate his expectation.

Tipping the entire contents of the bag onto the floor, I knelt down and rummaged through the perverted selection: two studded wrist bands, a matching dog collar, and what looked to be leather underpants with no back in them.

Kill, kill,

I want to kill me,

Hate, hate,

I hate me so,

Always the fool,

When I could've said no

Was it my fault?

Am I to blame?
Am I the one?
To feel so ashamed?

"Can I come in?" he asked in a breathy tone, like he'd been out for run. The sound of it knotted my stomach.

"Yeah," I squeaked out, utterly humiliated, standing in the centre of the elegant lounge; waiting for his inspection. I may as well have been nude, my attire, what little there was of it, only served to further my embarrassment.

As he entered the room, his face seemed to shine, his eyes sparkling like newly born stars and I could almost feel his gaze molesting me.

I wanted to vomit, my very soul begging for death, as he led the way up stairs and into small bedroom. *Help me mom*, I repeated over and over again in my mind.

The room was sparsely furnished, some half-filled bookshelves and standing at the foot of the single bed, a camera and tripod.

I suckled my coffee, which was already cold and bitter, in the hopes of buying myself time. Sensing my hesitation, Ropeman rested his hand on my shoulder, assuring me that "everything would be fine."

I shivered at his touch. Fear coursing through my body.

My chant now grew to include my dad, "*please, mum, dad . . . help me. Get me out of here, save me.*"

[107]

e instructed me to lay face down on the bed, as if I were sleeping. I could hear the click of the camera's shutter, my body felt rigid and tense, as if every muscle had ceased up.

"Maybe you should open your legs a bit more."

(Oh god, I don't want to do this.)

"That's better," he said, as I robotically followed his instructions.

I could feel the lens infiltrating my body.

"I think we've probably got enough shots like that now. Perhaps if you were turn over onto your back?"

"Can I go to the toilet first?"

"Of course, it's the door at the top of the stairs; you can't miss it."

I sat on the loo, staring at the cosmetics surrounding the bath. There were numerous bottles of shampoo, soaps, sponges, and a razor.

The small sharp blade caused me no pain as it slid across my wrist for the first time. I sat stone faced, gazing in amazement at the fresh wound, watching the blood escape from my body in perfect rhythm to the beat of my heart.

And there was no pain, none. I waited, but it never came.

The next time, I cut harder, much deeper.

There was still no pain.

My head began to spin and I felt clammy, but there was no pain . . . again and again I assaulted my forearm, finally throwing my head back inecstasy, reveling in celebration, perhaps this was the end of pain?

[108]

The sound of the monster beckoning extracted me from the fantasy,

"Simon. Simon! You okay in there?"

My eyes darted around the bathroom; no trace of blood, the razor still in its place amongst the cosmetics. There were no lacerations to my wrist or forearm.

"Yeah, just coming," I said listlessly as reality took a firm hold, clearing my head in an instant. The momentary relief my fantasy had provided now eluded me completely; it was not the end of my pain; it was only the beginning.

"Everything okay?"

"Yeah," I replied, averting my eyes.

I obediently took my place on the bed, and he immediately hit me with a sledgehammer of a request.

"If you could get a h**d on we'd only need a few more shots to get the money. Think you can manage that?"

I was fifteen.

I simply acknowledged with a nod of my head. Closing my eyes and gritting my teeth, I began fiddling with myself, trying desperately to visualise the pictures in the magazines stuffed under my bed, always acutely conscious of the camera shutter.

And then, just when I thought it couldn't get any worse.

"That's great Si'! Now, if there was a third hand in the shot, we'd have the cash in the bag. That'd be alright wouldn't it?"

Simon Palmer

(No, leave me alone you dirty fucking pig!)

I simply nodded again, completely dazed. My stomach churned and I felt sick. The camera's timer ran out, he squeezed me, and the picture was taken. A terrible moment captured forever, recording my initiation into child pornography and the beginning of my undoing.

I look in the mirror,

An' what do I see?

A face staring back,

That couldn't be me·

I look in the mirror,

An' what do I see?

A boy who is trapped,

Who longs to be free

Away from the terror,

Away from the pain,

Away from the feeling,

Of being to blame·

NIGHTMARES AND VIOLENCE

Just over two months had passed since the photo shoot, and I'd seen nothing of Ropeman. It was as though he'd vanished off the face of the earth, never to be seen again. But I was not that lucky, not by a long shot.

Somehow, I blocked out most of what happened in the tiny bedroom, and it was only in my dreams when it was at the forefront of my mind.

I'd started having a reoccurring nightmare in which Ropeman's hand is tightly wrapped around my penis, patiently waiting for the timer to run out. In my dream the camera's broken, and as I lay there looking up at him, he smiles that repugnant half-smirk of his. I longed to hear the click of the shutter signifying the end of the shot, but it never comes.

I also had more violent dreams of sexual brutality.

I find myself wandering through a beautiful forest on a bright summer's day. The birds are singing and there is a great sense of calmness, and I've never

felt so relaxed in my life. Breathing in deeply, my lungs fill with the crisp, clean, and
unpolluted country air.

Feeling an overwhelming desire to explore every inch of this glorious land, to capture and retain its natural purity, I follow the narrow footpath deeper into the woods ahead. The further I go, the more enthralled I become, and in my haste to reach an unknown goal, I trip on a protruding root and tumble to the ground, laughing before I fall.

With my fit of laughter all but over, I notice the sun has disappeared, and I'm entombed within an eerie darkness. There are four or five figures standing around me, silhouetted by the glare of the fiery torches in their hands.

No matter how hard I try, it's impossible to move. It seems as though all my muscles are frozen solid. As my attackers move closer, I realise they're all naked, sexually aroused, and then I see their faces; each is identical, it's Ropeman. They begin kicking me, and I can make out the voices of Stuart and Karen speaking into my mind, "You're one of us now, so enjoy the moment you little piece of shit."

The kicking stops as abruptly as it started, but I'm still in pain, awful pain, my chest and stomach burning. When I open my eyes, I realise I'm naked too. The burning continues and I cry out. Karen screeches loudly, "shut up!" And my eyes dart in every direction trying to source the origin of my suffering, and then I see it; my captors are ejaculating fire on me.

THE ROAD TO KINGFISHER

Morris was not to blame. He was just unlucky enough to be in the wrong place at the wrong time, and I was there waiting for him.

It was a Friday afternoon. I'd stopped caring whether I'd be put away and wagged school with Sean. We sniffed glue most of the day, and returned to the school at home time, hoping to find someone who'd "donate" their cigarettes to us. Poor old Morris came bounding around the corner, nearly knocking me over. You could see the fear sweep across his face, his mouth moving but no words came out.

"Hello wanker, got any fags?" I asked, widening my eyes in an attempt to scare him even more.

"No, I, I smoked 'em all at lunch."

"Fuck off." I took a step closer.

"I haven't! I smoked 'em all, honest!"

I took hold of the lapels of his blazer, "bollocks, don't lie to me you little prick!"

"Leave me alone Si', I aint got none!"

I punched him full in the face. He let out an agonising cry as his nose exploded blood and tears began to stream down his cheeks.

[113]

When he fell to the ground, I began brutally kicking him. He curled into a ball, attempting to avoid the swing of my boot. Morris was howling like a baby. With every kick I delivered the faces of Ropeman, Stuart, and Karen, flashed in my mind; and the clearer the pictures became, the more violently I kicked.

I could hear my name being called, but it sounded as if it were somewhere in the distance.

"Fuckin' hell Si', leave him! You're gonna kill the fucker!" I heard Sean's voice; no longer off in the distance, but shouting directly in my ear.

Somehow Sean managed to drag me away, tears now pouring from my eyes as well. We ran down the hill and across the road at the bottom, franticly dodging cars like frightened rabbits. With Sean still clutching my arm we sped down an alley and into the garden of a derelict house, my adrenaline pumping and the anger still very much in control.

"What the fuck did ya do that for?" I shouted, still readied for confrontation.

"Bollocks Si', you'd have killed the poor little cunt!"

I grabbed Sean by the collar and pulled his face close to mine, "You ever do somethin' like that again an' I'll fuckin' well do you an' all, d'you understand me?"

I let go of him and he fell to his knees, still gasping for air after all the running we'd just endured. Sean knew better than to argue with me, therefore nothing else was said.

[114]

We left the garden and peered around the corner; everything seemed quiet, so we casually began walking down the road. I asked if we were going to meet up on Monday morning, the usual place, at the entrance of the cemetery. He nodded, before turning on his heels, and we went our separate ways. I never saw Sean again.

It took me nearly an hour to walk home that afternoon, afraid of what would be waiting for me. Surely Morris had told a teacher or the coppers. I began to wonder if I'd gone too far this time.

No Police cars were visible as I turned the corner and into my road, perhaps they'd already been and gone?

I opened the front door as quietly as possible, and came face to face with my Father, "We've had your teacher on the phone, you've really done it this time lad!" he yelled, his face red with rage.

"Done what?" I replied, trying to sound casual.

"You know damn bloody well what you've done!"

"Have a nice day at school did you?" he asked loudly, his sarcasm more than apparent.

"What?"

"Don't give me all that, you aint been again have you? The social worker's coming to see you Monday morning. You deserve all you bloody get!"

Not wanting to listen any further, I pushed passed him and stomped up the stairs to my room. I searched franticly for some glue, looking under the bed, behind the chest of drawers, but there was none to be found anywhere. The only thing my search uncovered was a list of options I'd jotted down while planning to kill myself. Placing the paper in my pocket, I went out.

I was still unconvinced that Morris hadn't grassed me up, and I decided my best course of action would be to tell Stuart and Karen, hoping they could give me some advice.

Stuart listened intently before sitting back in his chair, "Well, you've fucked this one up aint ya?" I remained silent.

"Do you know how bad this other geezer is?" I could almost hear the cogs whirling around in his skull.

"No, but I definitely busted his conk."
Karen let out a snigger, to which Stuart gave her one of his, "shut the fuck up" looks. "It aint a fuckin' laughing matter!"

I wasn't sure what had set him off, until it dawned on me, he thought I was cracking a joke. My use of the word, "conk," had offended him, and I immediately corrected myself, "Sorry Stu', I meant his nose, I think I must've broke it."

"Well, what's done is done," he sighed, "Here's what you do; you've been going to school since court, right?"

"More or less, yeah."

"Right, when they ask, tell 'em you've been tryin', but this kid won't stop bullying yer and you'd gone back to school to tell the Headmaster why you never turned up. An' make sure you tell 'em you left it to home time coz you thought he'd 'ave gone home, an' you didn't wanna bump into him, say you were scared when you saw him and yer snapped, right?" I nodded again.

"Right, now fuck off home, say sorry to your old man and tell him the same story. It might sound better if he knows too."

Simon Palmer

MONDAY MORNING

The weekend had gone by without anything happening; I'd spent both Saturday and Sunday around Stuart and Karen's, but I was spared any abuse as their Daughter and her two children were down for the weekend. There weren't any arguments at home, although there was a bit of an atmosphere. My Dad hadn't bought the story of me being bullied, but once I turned on the waterworks his opinion changed, albeit only slightly.

I'd been told to stay in the house Monday morning, but I was gagging for a smoke and slipped out while no one was looking. I nipped to the local shop for some tobacco. I hadn't intended to stay out for any length of time; nor had making myself purposely late for the "meeting" even crossed my mind, but the more I thought about getting back, the more I became convinced something bad was going to happen. Even though it was the judge who'd threatened me with going into care, my Mother was constantly saying she was going to have my social worker, Bill Thackeray, put me in a boy's home, saying there were times she wished they'd never adopted me. These things were said in the heat of an argument, and I know the words held no meaning, both of my parents loved me, they were just frustrated, completely baffled by my horrid behaviour.

Bill pulled up in his battered green mini at around ten in the morning. I watched as he scuttled up the garden path, his image bringing an immediate smile to my face. His clothes were so typical of a social worker; the duffle coat, complete with wooden pegs for buttons, a leather satchel which looked like it was purchased on his graduation day. From the corner of his mouth dangled a roll-up made with liquorice cigarette papers.

As the meeting got under way, I felt the need to be rude and aggressive building. It wasn't something I could control, and the emotion always clouded my judgment. With every question Bill threw at me, I had an unreasonable response ready, chucking in some choice swear words for good measure. I ranted about how "no one ever listened to me," and of how I "hated living in this fuckin' house!"

Mum, by this time completely fed up with my behaviour, retaliated by telling Bill she wanted me out of the family home, adding that I was making her ill.

"Fuck the lot of yer. You're all a bunch of cunts that can rot in fuckin' hell!"

I jumped to my feet, threw my cup at the wall and walked out, shouting that I wished she'd died on the operating table. Mum had gone under the knife a while back, but my ability to cause emotional pain far outweighed my loyalties, my cruel streak knew no boundaries.

[120]

Losing the Hate

With my rage controlling my actions, and my heart filled with unrelenting resentment, I decided that it was time for me to leave home.

Simon Palmer

A REQUEST FOR SOME "WORK"

Standing opposite the school, I quickly darted over the Zebra crossing as soon as Ropeman came into my view.

"Hi Sir!" I said enthusiastically trying to appear cheerful.

"Hello young man, you ok?"

"Yeah I'm alright. I was, I was wondering, do you? Can we do some more work?"

He smiled.

"Well, this is a surprise I must say," he looked around, making sure no one was in earshot, "I don't see why not, when were you thinking of ?"

"Dunno, soon as possible really. I, I really need the money."

"Why. What's up?" he asked, his expression was one of concern and it surprised me.

"There's a, err, I've seen some trousers I really want an' me Mum won't buy 'em." The lie rolled off my tongue with ease, but Ropeman didn't care why I was there anyways. Without further prompting, he suggested we meet outside the swimming baths on Saturday afternoon.

It didn't occur to me that the "sessions" with Ropeman could get worse. My only concern was getting away, and this was the only means I had to do it.

Although it did cross my mind that the money I stood to earn wouldn't last long. Perhaps I would join the homeless kids living London's West End, resort to stealing as means of support?

And as I plotted my escape, I also fantasized about my inevitable return, picturing the faces of everyone who had interfered with my childhood as I exacted my revenge.

I'll brave your wickedness,

I'll brave my pain,

You'll give me some money,

An' never see me again·

Take your pictures,

Satisfy your need,

Destroy my life,

An' feed your greed·

In years to come,

When you've forgotten my name,

The past will return,

An' you'll play my game·

I'll become a man,

An' learn how to fight,

Losing the Hate

I'll enter your life,
An' make things right·
You'll lose your job,
An' maybe a wife,
How great it will feel,
To destroy your life·
People like you,
Will never be free,
Chained to your sickness,
By victims like me·
But for now,
I'll brave your wickedness,
I'll manage my pain,
You'll give me the money,
An' never see me again·

Simon Palmer

SHOPPING WITH A MONSTER

I was overcome with paranoia while waiting for Ropeman to make an appearance. The crowd of people innocently milling around made me feel uncomfortable. When someone inadvertently glanced in my direction I was convinced they knew exactly what I was up to.

After sticking a fag in the corner of my mouth, I realised I'd forgotten my lighter, the paranoia had all but consumed me, and there was no way I was going to ask anyone for a light.

Startled by the sound of hearing my name being called, I looked for the source, it was Ropeman. I moved quickly towards his car, and got in.

"Sorry I'm a bit late, but I'm afraid we've got a bit of a problem."

My heart sank.

"What's up don't the bloke want any?"

"No, no, nothing like that. It's just that the house we went to before is unavailable and there's nowhere else we can go."

[127]

I couldn't believe it. After preparing myself mentally for another session, making my escape plans, now this? I'd be going home to more arguments, which was bad enough, but I could feel my hopes of getting away from Stuart and Karen slipping through my fingers. One more session with Ropeman seemed a small price to pay for my freedom.

"The best I can do is Tuesday morning I'm afraid, think you can bunk off school again?"

"Yeah course," I replied, "I guess I'll 'ave to get the trousers in the week."

He patted me on the knee

"Tell you what; you got anything planned for this evening?"

"Nothin' much, why?"

He asked if I fancied going to Carnaby St, saying we might find a nice pair of punky type trousers there, and offered to buy me something to eat too.

The car came to a halt in a tiny road just off of Oxford Street. Ropeman led me through a series of narrow winding alleyways, until we finally entered the most fashionable street in London. He told me to go ahead and have a wander.

I was thrilled! There were so many shops to choose from, and it was especially exciting because many of them contained memorabilia reminiscent of the punk explosion that rocked the nation during the late 70's.

"I'm just going to nip off for a bit; I'll be half an hour, tops. Make sure you stay in this area won't you? Otherwise you'll get lost."

I promised not to stray so he would be able to find me upon his return.

I was alone in the heart of London, Ropeman had vanished into the throng of demonic shoppers, all intent on spending money they didn't have on over priced rubbish. It would have been easy to simply slip away, meet up with other runaways and begin my new life. The only obstacle standing in my way was money, with no cash it would be impossible to eat or drink; and the cigarettes I had were sure to be gone by morning.

Deciding it was best to wait until Tuesday, I began my search for the ultimate pair of trousers. It was very important they be the right ones, and I would only be happy if I could actually visualise Johnny Rotten wearing them.

My quest ended as soon as I entered the second shop, my eyes spotted them straight away, hanging on a clothing rail in all their magnificent glory! They were tartan bondage, and I was already picturing myself strutting down the road like the megastar I was so desperate to become.

A hand rested on my shoulder and I spun on my heels, not quite knowing who to expect standing there; it was Ropeman.

"I see you've found what you were looking for."
"Yeah, they're fuckin' awesome aint they."
"Maybe you should try them on for size?"
The excitement rushed through my body, "Can I?"
"Of course, that's why where're here isn't it?"
Ropeman summoned a young female shop assistant.

Simon Palmer

Her hair was bright pink, which looked fantastic against the heavy black make-up dominating her face. She was wearing skin tight PVC trousers, and her torn white T-shirt must have had at least two hundred safety pins attached.

I asked if I could try on my prized find, and she led me into the rear of the shop, pointing towards the changing rooms. I remember taking a sly glance at her bum as she walked ahead of me.

Who would have believed that a simple item of clothing could totally transform someone's perception of themselves? When I emerged from the dressing room, I was thoroughly convinced, that I, Simon James Palmer, had morphed into the most hated punk rocker ever to dare walk on God's Earth.

Who are you?
Where are you?
 Look at me,
An' what I am·
Stand in my way,
An' I'll knock you down,
I don't give a fuck,
If you wear a crown,
Coz I am Sye,
An' I know what I am·
You look at me,

Losing the Hate

An' shake your head,
You think to yourself,
He'll soon be dead·
I'm told an' told,
I'm a big disgrace
,Just you wait,
I'll push shit in yer face·
I don't give a toss,
You can scream an' shout,
Coz I am Sye,
An' I know what I am·
You can tear me apart
You can kick me down,
But watch your back,
Coz I'll stand my ground·
I'll come back,
When you're alone,
Ruin your world,
An' you're perfect home·
When you're dead,
I'll sing so loud,
I am Sye,
An' I am what I am·

Simon Palmer

CARDS ON THE TABLE

With the purchase complete we made our way back through the narrow alleys. I tried to catch a glimpse of myself in every shop window we passed; proud of the way the trousers made me stand out from the crowd.

Once the bustle of the West End traffic was behind us, I asked Ropeman if he would drop me at my Aunt and Uncle's house, saying I'd get a ride back home with my Mum and Dad.

"No problem, where do they live?"

"If you drop me by the gasworks on the Old Kent road, I can walk from there."

He patted me on the knee.

"Are you pleased with the trousers?"

"Yeah, they're fuckin' cool!"

"You will be careful won't you? You know you can't tell anyone I bought them for you, don't you?"

"Yeah, I know," I smiled, "I'll think of somethin', they won't believe whatever I tell them anyway."

Ropeman offered to rent the Sex Pistols' film for Tuesday, saying after we got work out of the way, we could watch it.

"Yeah. Brill'."

I told him the gasworks were coming up, and he stopped the car a bit further off.

"You're not gonna forget about Tuesday now are you?"

I shook my head, "Course not, 10 o'clock outside the railway station."

Again he reached for my knee, but this time he gave it a squeeze.

"There's a good lad."

The atmosphere in his tiny car suddenly changed, and within seconds, Ropeman laid his cards on the table.

"If I'm not able to hire the movie we'll still do the work."

"Yeah course, its already sorted," I replied.

He smiled, "And we'll have some sex, yes?"

I was fifteen.

"Yeah," I responded, slightly shaking my head hoping the words would somehow fall out of my ears and onto ground where I could stomp them beneath my feet. "Have a little sex?" Was that actually what the filthy fat bastard had said?

I briefly managed to regain my composure, just long enough to get out of the car and across the street. The hunger pangs from not eating suddenly vanished, and my legs threatened to give out from under me.

[134]

Losing the Hate

Without warning images began flashing in my mind, a slide-show of memories which until now had been neatly tucked away; only surfacing in my dreams.

Simon Palmer

TUESDAY MORNING

By the time Tuesday rolled around, the commitment to my planned escape had been reaffirmed by a few more go rounds with Stuart and Karen. My survival, I was absolutely sure, depended on it.

Feeling desperate to free myself from their bondage, and becoming ever more fearful of the simmering rage within me, I fooled myself into believing I had misunderstood Ropeman's words. And if not, I rationalized, then it was merely a joke which I had misconstrued.

In any case, I was ready and waiting outside the station when Ropeman's car pulled alongside me. His spongy cheeks ballooned from behind the windscreen as a self-satisfied smirk passed over his face. He seemed surprised to see me.

"Morning young man, all set then?"

"Yeah."

"Good lad, I managed to get the film."

"Cool."

"What did you tell your Mum and Dad about the trousers? They don't know I got them do they?"

"Na, they think I nicked 'em from somewhere."

"Oh dear, still never mind. We both know you didn't steal them."

"It don't matter anyhow, they'll get over it. Can I have a fag?"

"Of course, just wind the window down."

By the time we arrived at the house in Catford, my nerves were on edge. Ropeman seemed more enthusiastic than usual, and as we made our up the path leading to the familiar structure, I began sweating profusely.

My heart was pounding and my body was overcome with a terrible fear, but I obediently followed his lead.

Was this swine of a human being actually planning to have sex with me?

I forced back the images of such a thing. Surely this was just another nightmare?

When Ropeman instructed me to shut the door, panic set in. My breathing became laboured, and the tiny gasping breaths I managed to inhale where not providing the oxygen to keep me from getting dizzy.

Completely oblivious, Ropeman cheerfully chirped out,

"If you'd like to go straight upstairs, I'll go and get a pot of coffee going. Would you like some toast or something?"

"Just coffee please," I responded, struggling to make my up the stairs.

"Ok. You know where the bedroom is, I'll be up with the coffee in a minute."

As my hand reached for the door knob, he yelled, "Oh, I've put a few things on the bed that you might want to try on, see what you think!"

The camera and tripod still pointed towards the single bed. A small pile of skimpy leather clothing was neatly spread out on the pillow.

"The coffee's nearly ready. I thought we'd watch the film before doing the photos, how does that sound?"

"Yeah, cool," I said gratefully, thinking perhaps it was a reprieve. Maybe Ropeman was having second thoughts?

He gently prompted me to sit on the edge of the bed.

"What's bothering you Si'?"

Ropeman was standing above me, one hand on my shoulder, leaning into my face.

"Do you think I'm a poof?" I blurted out, backing away from the assault of his warm breath against my skin.

"What?" he looked puzzled.

"Do you think I'm gay or something?"

"No, of course not! Is that what's bothering you?"

My lips began quivering forcing my gaze to the floor.

"Yeah, a little bit."

He put his arm around me, "Don't be daft, it's just a way of making a bit of money, that's all. Tell you what; let's watch the film and we'll see how you feel when it's finished. If you still don't feel up to it, we can always do the photos another day, sound good?"

[139]

The relief I felt threatened to vibrate my body, "yeah, ok."

Ropeman left the room, only to re-enter within seconds, "I've just had the most fantastic idea; how about we film ourselves watching the movie?"

I wasn't sure what he was getting at, sounded rather stupid to me. But I was too relieved, and still somewhat dazed to say anything.

"Look, I've got one of the school's video cameras in the boot," he continued, "why don't we set it up on the tripod and record ourselves. That way you don't have to worry about getting embarrassed posing for any photographs."

The idea of not doing any pictures did appeal to me, but in truth, a tiny knot formed in my stomach, something just didn't feel right.

"Alright then," I said.

"Great! You get the film running, and I'll just nip out to the car and get the camera," he said in an exuberant tone which puzzled me, but once again, my emotions were too off-balance to think straight. And even with a clear head, I could have never predicted what was in store for me.

I enjoyed his absence, and started to relax a little. But I had to make a conscious effort not to think about the things which had occurred the last time I found myself confined in the tiny room.

Following his directives, I set my attention to the portable television sitting on a table at the foot of the bed, and slid the video cassette in the machine atop.

As if perfectly synchronized, when Ropeman stepped back in the room, the knot returned to my stomach, but the pain almost caused me to buckle over.

"I err; I'm not too sure about this."

Ropeman sighed loudly, "Don't worry; there's nothing to be afraid of. It'll be ok, trust me."

Without waiting for a reply, he removed his shirt and sat on the bed. Edging his body backwards, until he was almost spread out. "C'mon Si', take your shirt off and join me, you're missing the film."

A feeling surfaced from deep within, and I suddenly felt like a young child, small and utterly insignificant.

He coaxed me into using his chest as a backrest, and encompassed my upper body in his arms, resting his sweaty palms on my bare belly.

As the Sex Pistols began to pump out their version of the classic Little Richard song, Johnny B Good, Ropeman began to caress my stomach. My body automatically tensed, and the pervert whispered into my ear, "its ok, I'm just doing it for the tape, try and relax."

"Ok, sorry," I said, struck almost immediately be the irony of having apologized to the dirty bastard.

"You're not going to hurt me are you?"

"Don't be silly, I wouldn't dream of it."

I closed my eyes, swallowing back the bile continually making its way to my throat, and the urge to evacuate my bowels became more persistent as the sound of his breathing changed.

"Now then, why don't you turn around and lay on top of me?"

[141]

I wanted to cry, the tiny muscles in my face twitching back an onslaught of tears, as my head shook ever so slightly back and forth.

It was all the resistance I could offer, the terror paralysing me into submission, as he pulled me closer. I could feel his hot putrid breath on my face. He was panting, and had started to tremble. Without warning, his hand grasped the back of my neck. I struggled, but he was too strong. And before I could register his intentions, he thrust his tongue deep into my mouth.

A sickening sensation came overcame me, when he began pushing me towards his waist, his hips gyrating in anticipation, as he forced my mouth towards his p***s. With my face only inches away, he suddenly groaned . . . it was over.

It was suggested that I go "clean myself up."

I went. I sobbed rather than cried.

I scrubbed my face, tears streaming down my checks.

I scrubbed again, my face burning, my body shaking uncontrollably.

The tears had to stop, before he heard.

I scrubbed my face again.

My heart beating fast.

And then....

"Simon?"

I ignored him.

The demon called me again.

I still gave no reply.

Then I heard the footsteps, followed by a knock on the door.

"Simon. Is everything alright?"

[142]

I had no choice but answer, "yeah, I'm, I'm fine. Be out in a minute."

"Good, I'll put some more coffee on."

I breathed a sigh of relief at the sound of his heavy footfalls on the stairs.

When I was sure he had gone, I started to sob all over again. A lump forming in my throat as the reality of going back into the bedroom set in.

Wiping my eyes, I scrubbed at my face one last time.

But I still felt so incredibly dirty.

As soon as I ventured into the hall, I bumped straight into Ropeman.

"There you are, all cleaned up then fella?" he asked, gesturing for me to cross the upper landing.

"Yeah," I replied, wishing I could summon the courage to knock the coffee tray from his hands, and kick the sick bastard down the stairs, but instead I walked to the bedroom.

"We've more or less got the money in the bag after that bit of filming; you were very good matey," he said following me into the room.

I couldn't believe my ears, what did he mean by "more or less?'

Please God; don't let him do that to me again.

Ropeman poured some coffee, "You really have surprised me young man. You're quite the little actor aren't you?"

I wasn't acting, you evil fucking pig.

"Dunno, am I?"

He handed me the drink, "You most certainly are, now then, shall we get the last bit of filming done? Then we can settle down and watch the movie."

The words were too difficult to string together to make any sense, "I thought.., you said.., can we, hadn't we.., err, finish…, aint it err, finished."

He frowned at me, as if I'd done something naughty in class and he was about to discipline me, "now come on, you got your trousers. When I dropped you Saturday you said we'd have some sex. "

I began to panic, "But you," before I could finish, he cut me off, shooting me a stern look, before saying, "that's enough, now try some of those things on and get back on the bed."

Without further protest I robotically put on the leather underpants, the ones with no backing, as the predator stood by and watched.

"Right, if you can lie on top of me again, but this time I want you to writhe around a bit," he said, his face flushing. The trembling tone in his voice set off an alarm in my mind.

"And when I give the nod, if you can sit up and sort of straddle my waist that'd be great."

I had no idea that he was going to be naked.

And I soon found out why the underpants had no backing.

An hour later he was driving me back to school.

"You've done very well today, here, take this before anyone sees." He thrust thirty pounds into my hand; I took the money.

I needed the toilet.
I felt sick, and the pain . . . the pain was unbearable.
My inner shorts were wet.
He was still inside me . . . and the pain was unbearable.
I wanted to die!
And I was dirty. I would always be dirty . . . . the pain
was unbearable.

Simon Palmer

STEPPING STONE TO KINGFISHER

After the rape, my home life fell to an all time low, rock bottom in fact. The violence grew, with me threatening my Mother and elder sister, Kelly, as well as becoming brave enough to extend the threats towards my Father. Even my visits to Stuart and Karen's became less frequent, and when I realised they were hanging around outside my house, I began to go out via the fence at the bottom of my garden, which gave me access to the council flats beyond.

Finally, and without any warning, my social worker visited me at school to discuss "a change of environment." As a result of my constant disruptive behaviour, and my inability to adhere to the basic reasonable rules my parents rightly demanded, it was decided things would be better all round if I was removed from the family home and placed with foster parents for an indefinite period of time.

I never liked Bill from the start, and in some ways I saw him as a threat to my although nothing was said, I knew he could see through the façade. The thought of him ripping the mask from my face petrified me. There was no way I was going to allow him to expose the mixed up confused child hiding beneath my tough exterior.

When we arrived in Swanley, I wasn't sure if my erratic heartbeat was due to excitement or fear. Bill led me to the front door of a modest semi and rang the bell; dogs immediately began to bark. An overweight lady opened the door and invited us inside, leading the way into the lounge where we were greeted by five children and two adults. They scanned me as if I'd just beamed down from outer space.

Bill introduced me to the woman, Joan Dodd, who in turn presented her five children, each smiling brightly as their names were mentioned. The two adults were Joan's brother Tom, and a good friend by the name of Angela.

The house rules were outlined, and I agreed to abide by their expectations, should it be decided that I was to stay. My only question was whether or not I'd be allowed to smoke, to which the answer was a stern, non negotiable no!

The entire family attended a Judo club almost every night, as well as competitions at the weekends, and I would be encouraged to take an active part in this. My reply to this was a stern, non negotiable no! Sport was never a friend of mine and there was absolutely no way I wanted to make its acquaintance now. My mind couldn't think of anything worse than grappling around on a matt with a complete stranger; it seemed to serve no purpose whatsoever and I wanted no part of it.

After about an hour or so of irrelevant pleasantries, Bill indicated it was time to make the drive back to South London, and so we said our goodbyes before trundling off down the road in his battered old Mini, leaving behind the tongues that were bound to be wagging.

It was mid afternoon the following day when I was summoned to the school secretary's office; my Mother was apparently on the phone and wished to speak with me. I ran down the desolate corridor to the office.

"Simon." My Mother's voice sounded very anxious.

"Yeah, what's goin' on?"

"Bill's been to see me this morning, he's keen for you to go and stay in Swanley for a while."
I could tell she was holding back tears.

"You could've told me when I got home. When am I goin'?"

My Mum paused for a moment before answering, "he wants you to go today. He's gonna pick you up from school shortly."

"What? What about all my stuff? Me clothes an' everything."

Panic was setting in; I had no idea any of this was actually going to happen.

"Bill picked your stuff up this morning."

My response became very defensive, I was hurt, "Don't 'ave much choice then do I? See you around sometime!" I put the phone down. The hurt, as often happens, turned to rage. The thought that my Mother's heart was breaking never even crossed my mind.

KINGFISHER BECOMES IMMINENT

Bill picked me up from school shortly after my conversation with Mum, and that evening I began a new life with a family that meant absolutely nothing to me. I did not, and would not fit in! They were not my parents, and I made damn sure these people were completely aware of that.

Joan tried to entice me into starting my schooling at the local comprehensive, but there was no way I was about to change schools, insisting I travel by train to South London. Luckily, Bill was on my side with regards to this matter and he arranged a weekly travel card.

It was very important for me to stay in my local area, and having the use of my train pass at weekends was a welcome bonus, allowing me the freedom to hang around with Peter and Mark, rather than putting up with the tedious Judo competitions. I'd often tell Joan that Peter's Mum had agreed to put me up for the night, usually on Saturdays.

[151]

In actuality I was attending all night parties, getting blind drunk and smoking heaps of cannabis, all of which was usually funded by petty crime.

I never really got on too well with Joan's husband, Mike, who was very set in his ways and couldn't quite get his head around the way I chose to dress. Nothing was ever actually said, it was just something we were both aware of. But he was a very reasonable man and never went out of his way to make life hard for me.

There were some rather volatile situations during my stay in Swanley, one of which was the marriage of Joan and Mike's elder son, Gerry. It was a formal church wedding followed by a huge reception at a local hall. I'd refrained from wearing my usual clobber, instead, sporting a shirt and tie, (which was completely my choice).

The alcohol began to flow, and with Joan and Mike busy mingling amongst the many guests, no one thought to monitor how much I was drinking. In no time, my legs began to bend like rubber and I crashed in a heap onto the crowded dance floor, drunk as a skunk.

How I got home was a total mystery, however, I do remember slouching on the sofa next to Joan, a string of four letter words flowing from my lips, and spitting on the floor; eventually Mike put me to bed.

The next thing I knew it was early morning; a thousand little men with hammers banging away in my head. It didn't take me too long to realise I was lying in a large, smelly pool of sick, and, while the rest of the house continued to sleep, I crept to the bathroom, cleaned myself up as best I could and left for the railway station. I had no interest in being around when my foster carers woke to discover the unsavoury contents of my bed.

Arriving in Catford at around eight-thirty with no money in my pocket, I decided to take the short walk to Stuart and Karen's house. I hung around on the corner in the hope Karen would eventually appear for the morning paper. And sure enough, before I knew it, I saw her strolling along the road, calling to her as she drew closer, "Karen! It's me, you alright?"
We walked to the local newsagent and I told her what happened.

"You'll have to go back, you know that don't ya?"

"Fuck that. I aint goin' back to that shithole."

"Well what'll yer do then? You can't stay with me an' Stu."

After a bit of pondering, she gave me a tenner and told me to wait for her in the café next to the library, saying she may be able to sweet talk a friend into putting me up for a while. "And make sure no one sees you!" she called out, as I walked away.

Karen entered the "greasy spoon" café just as I was finishing a hearty fry up. She explained that a friend of hers had agreed to put me up for a few days.

The woman's name was Maggie, and while she appeared very nice, it soon became apparent that the evening was to bring a fresh wave of suggestive talk about Karen and myself. Unbeknown to me, Karen had already been talking with her friend about how she'd inadvertently fallen in love with me. Her plan was to

[153]

leave Stuart, and start a new life with me the minute I turned sixteen.

"Why don't you both move right away? There's plenty of people I can put you in touch with in Liverpool."

Karen shook her head, "He'd come lookin' for us, an' Simon an' me would both get a bash."

Didn't I have any fucking say in all of this?

"He'd give up after a while wouldn't he?" continued Maggie, "Lets face it, how'd he know to look in that direction?"

They were deciding my fate without considering that I might have an opinion, speaking as if I wasn't even in the room. Maggie looked at me, almost in surprise, as if I'd just appeared from a magical cloud of smoke.

"You'd move to Liverpool with Karen wouldn't yer?" Her gaze fixed on my eyes.

"Yeah, course." I lied.

Maggie continued with her warped plan, "there you go, and stay over tonight; Stuart doesn't know you're here does he?"

"Nah, he don't even know where you live."

"That's settled then," said Maggie, standing up, "I'll go an' get some dinner on. Think there's some lagers in the fridge Si, d'you want one?"

"Yeah, cool."

Later that evening, Karen began her advance, trying desperately to physically arouse me. I made one excuse after the next, telling her anything that came to mind, and going so far as to claim it was my fear of being caught by the authorities. Clearly none of it was true, and sadly for me, she knew it.

"Don't take me for a mug Simon!"

I stood my ground, "I aint. I'm just worried about things," and without asking, helped myself to her cigarettes.

"You're taking the fuckin' piss, my fags are okay aint they? But when I want something from you it's a different bloody story! And what about that tenner this morning? You forgotten about that?"

"I'm worried about me Mum."

"What?"

"I'm worried that me Mum's gonna be gettin' upset about where I might be."

She glared at me, "Excuses, its always bloody excuses with you!"

The battle raged on, and when I thought I could no longer suppress my rage, I succumbed to her demands, rationalising that it was the lesser of two evils. Before the onset of her advance, I'd already decided to leave anyways, hoping if I showed up at Social Services, Bill might still be willing to help me sort out my life.

Simon Palmer

KINGFISHER; A NEW START

As things turned out it, it was two days later that I finally journeyed out to see Bill Thackeray; eventually claiming that I was popping out to call my Mother, just to let her know I was okay and not to worry about me.

Within an hour of leaving Maggie's flat I was on a bus, using the money Karen had given me for the phone box to pay for my fare.

I found myself patiently waiting in the offices of the local authority which had long since become my second home. Bill walked through the internal door, and my fear of a severe telling off instantly vanished.

The look on his face was more one of concern than the rage I expected. It was clear; the man genuinely cared for my welfare, far more than his superiors expected of him. I opened up, telling him what a toll leaving home had really taken, explaining I didn't fit in at the foster home, and how I wanted to learn to look after myself.

Finally asking, if with my sixteenth birthday fast approaching, it might be possible to move into my own flat?

"Wait in here for a minute," he said, leading me into a private consultation room.

"I won't be long."

Four or five cigarettes later, Bill flung the door open, a smile plastered across his face. "How'd you feel about living in a pre-independence unit?"

Puzzlement attacked me with a ferociousness that filled my body with excitement and unleashed a swarm of butterflies in the pit of my tummy.

Kingfisher Square was a few miles away in Deptford. Bill explained it was an establishment set up to prepare young people leaving council care to learn to cope with the complexities of adulthood.

There were always two staff members on duty, these individuals would teach us the ropes, filling out applications for work or government training schemes, teaching us to cook and budget money In short, with their help we would learn to become responsible adults.

The council would provide £9 a week for my food budget in addition to supplying the "basics," milk, bread, tea and coffee.

On Sundays a roast dinner would be prepared, with the assistance of all the residents. Initially, it all sounded too good to be true, I almost felt as though it was an elaborate con, but the arrangements were made almost immediately, and for the first time in many years, I had some hope, some concrete evidence that I was not doomed, fated to be unhappy for the rest of my life.

We were greeted by a female member of the staff named Caz. She immediately made me feel extremely welcome. Shortly after the formalities, we were given a guided tour of the building, including where I would be sleeping. As we followed her up the stairs, I couldn't stop myself from gazing at her rear.

"You'll be sharing a room with Robert while you're on stage one, but you'll get a room of your own as soon as the team decides you've learnt enough to move on to stage two," she said, flicking her wavy auburn hair away from her face with her delicate long fingers. I thought she was absolutely beautiful.

There were three stages to the program at Kingfisher; the first consisted of learning all aspects of budgeting, as well as nutrition. Maintaining a varied and healthy diet was paramount to moving on to stage two. Caz was to be my "link worker," closely monitoring my progress in these areas.

Stage two was more intense, I would be expected to live on my own and be given a lot more financial freedom, but I couldn't expect to reach stage two until my schooling was complete, and I was actively seeking work or training.

Once stage three was achieved it was a waiting game, only hanging on until the council offered me a flat, although I couldn't expect that to happen until I was at least seventeen.

After seeing the room I would be sharing, we returned to the office to sign the necessary forms for my new life to begin. Bill would be dropping off the belongings I had left in Swanley the following morning.

Caz introduced me to me Mark, another member of the staff team, before taking me food shopping. She gave me the money and took a back seat, saying she wanted to see if I was able to buy a balanced diet.

I was becoming an adult, and before long I would be the one calling the shots. Finally free of Karen and Stuart, not to mention that swine Ropeman, my life was now well on course, and I felt terribly happy.

DRUGS, DRINK, AND SELF LOATHING

The first few months went swimmingly well. There were no clashes between me and the other five residents, and I'd been allowed to shop for myself following my initial trip with Caz. Even the relationship with my family was back on a fairly even keel.

As soon as the time came for me to leave school everything changed. Between what the state paid me and my food allocation, I was receiving £35 a week. After paying £4.50 board and lodging, the rest of the money was my mine to spend.

I began to drink heavily and it wasn't long before I made friends who were keen to sell me as much cannabis as I could afford. As my drug and alcohol abuse grew, the unemployment money was no longer enough to cover the lifestyle I'd become accustomed to, and I became very aggressive towards the staff at Kingfisher.

To make my money go further, I started drinking very strong lager with a volume of 9%, only

[161]

returning home when I was out of drink or spoiling for a fight.

The more the staff tried to understand why my behaviour had taken such a dramatic turn, the more I rebelled against them, threatening to run away or smash up furniture. When my threats centred on violence towards whichever staff member I was arguing with, Bill informed me that they'd been instructed to call the police, telling me my adverse behaviour would no longer be tolerated.

The anger inside me continued to escalate and my alcohol consumption remained astronomically high. Feeling unable to release the tension coursing through my veins, I started to self harm in a manner which never happened before; taking kitchen knives to my forearm and really cutting myself in a disturbing way. I'd butcher my arm, hacking rather than cutting, causing gapping wounds that pumped rather than oozed blood. The hatred I'd often shown towards others was now turning inward; and my greatest wish was that death would take me away.

Things got so bad I was being taken to the local hospital two or three times a week to be stitched up. The casualty staff demanded an explanation as to why I was being allowed to hurt myself whilst still under the supervision of council care workers.

It was decided all the kitchen knives were to be kept under lock and key, and if I needed to peel some spuds or cut some meat, it would be done for me, but short of locking me up, there was pretty much little else they could do. Caz continued to try and help. She was genuinely concerned, but I really didn't have any interest in sorting things out. The self destruct button in my head was now activated, and there was little anyone could do to help.

As well as self harming, I reacquainted myself with sniffing glue only now I no longer did it privately, thinking nothing of sitting in the communal lounge with my "bag," waiting for a reaction. When none came, I was more than happy to just get high, revisiting the euphoric world which had welcomed me only a few years before.

I remember one situation in particular, when I pushed my luck to its limits with the officer in charge. His name was Malcolm, a very experienced social worker, being in the job for over ten years. I'd decided to glue sniff in the lounge, desperate to create an argument with him.

Sure enough it was only a matter of minutes before he entered the sitting room, demanding I hand over the bag of Evostick. I told him to fuck off; and he did. Thinking I'd won the battle, I strutted into the kitchen, where another member of the staff was making a hot drink Proud of my apparent victory, I boasted, "he's a fuckin' good social worker aint he? Couldn't even get the glue off me, wanker."

The residents present looked at me in disbelief, and the staff member, a black guy called Les, smiled at me and simply said, "D'you want to talk about it Simon?"

I paced around the dinning table, inhaling the bag of glue, laughing hysterically between breaths, knowing I looked absolutely insane.

[163]

"Simon, you don't need that stuff," continued Les, "why don't you come into the quiet room and have a chat?"

I begrudgingly followed Les, doing a shit job of imitating his swagger for the benefit of no one in particular.

"Fuck it, what d'you want me to talk about then?"

Unbeknown to me, Malcolm had called the police, and just as I handed Les my bag, two officers came running towards me. I legged it through the lounge and out the back door, making it halfway across the garden, before being caught. A torrent of abuse flew from my mouth and I began to kick out at my captors. They managed to get the handcuffs on me and I spat in their faces.

"You bunch of fuckin' pricks, get yer fuckin' hands off me you dirty cunts!"

I was frog marched out of the building and shoved into the back of the van, with Les following.

"Calm down Simon, we'll get it all sorted out at the police station. Don't worry, it'll all be fine."

Deptford "nick" was a mere stones throw from Kingfisher, and so it was only a matter of minutes before I found myself sitting in the custody suite.

Following a search the cops also found a small quantity of cannabis in my jacket pocket, together with some "poppers," (amyl nitrate).

I'd discovered poppers a few months prior while browsing one of the many adult shops in London's West End. The arresting officer took the substances away and I was left sitting with Les on a bench running along the back wall of the room.

"What's up mate? You've really got to sort things out buddy, why d'you keep doing these things to yourself?"

I was crying.
I was scared.
And I hated me.

"I just fuckin' hate myself Les, just wanna fuckin' die."

My voice was raised and a few of the policemen milling around glanced over, probably concerned I was going to kick off again. But Les carried an air of confidence, it was clear he had things under control, so they refrained from intervening.

When Les instructed me to stay put and left, the minutes seemed like hours. I was convinced they were going to charge me for possession at the very least, if not resisting arrest, and in all honesty, that's not what was bothering me. I was more concerned that my stay at Kingfisher was in jeopardy.

Finally, Les returned together with the arresting officer. It was decided I would only be cautioned, but it was made clear, next time would definitely be a different story.

Simon Palmer

CHANGE OF DIRECTION

Over the following six months, I finally began getting my act together, my encounter with the police made this easier for me than expected. In addition, Malcolm informed me that the only way I could avoid having to leave Kingfisher was to stop using both drink and drugs. I was also expected to enlist in some kind of training course, or gain full time employment.

It didn't take me long to locate a Y.T.S organization, happy to offer me a two year training course. I would be working within an adventure playground environment, as well as learning different aspects of young people at play. I was told it was a necessary part of the training program to attend college one day a week to acquire a two year foundation course in play leadership. And although it all sounded pretty daunting, I found the challenge exciting.

As well as with working with children, the job involved the building of tyre swings, climbing frames, and varying structures consisting of scrap wood donated by, or purchased from local traders.

[167]

Sandy Combes, my immediate boss, decided it would be beneficial to incorporate a pet's corner within the playground, and I was selected to be in charge of the new project.

A mini bus was hired and we took the children on a short trip to the Isle of Dogs in East London, to visit a city farm. We were hoping to acquaint the children with a variety of farm animals they had never seen before. And as a side note, it would help us decide which animals to include in our playground project.

The children had tremendous fun, and after gaining some invaluable information from the farm staff, we decided to buy two goats and a few rabbits for "my" pet's corner.

The following four months saw me, together with a gang of dedicated teenagers, digging and planting grass seeds. Our time was also spent building adequate shelter in a far corner of the playground. The end result was fantastic; we had succeeded in creating our own miniature city farm, with limited funding, but a lot of heart. It was an overwhelming success, and it filled me with a pride I had not experienced before.

A tuck shop was set up, run by a lovely local lady, the proceeds going towards the purchase and maintenance of the animals.

After a lot of hard work, the goats finally turned up, along with the local newspaper to cover the event. Everyone involved in this labour of love, including myself, made the front page of that week's edition. My life was suddenly a very happy one.

The dramatic changes left me feeling very content with the way things were panning out, and although there were still many issues which needed addressing, I continued to strive for success in becoming a mature adult.

All of my positive responses to continuing the program at Kingfisher were bringing me ever closer to my dream, gaining the independence of living alone. And within a matter of months, the letter from the council landed on the matt; my offer of a one bedroom flat had arrived.

After receiving a £500 leaving care grant, and getting superb support from my Mum and Dad, I moved into my new home with nothing but admiration from everyone.

And then it all changed.

Simon Palmer

MISTAKES

In the third and final part of my story, I would like to speak of the mistakes I've made through the course of my adult life. There is a lot of pain and emotional torment I have managed to keep locked away for many years, but I honestly don't know if my short comings are a result of not confronting my issues, or if the misfortunes I've created are just down to me and me alone.

In many ways the pain I've experienced during my adulthood has been much more arduous than the experiences I was unfortunate enough to have had as a child.

Simon Palmer

PART THREE
VICTIM ? OR MONSTER?

Simon Palmer

Losing the Hate

I gently opened the bedroom door trying desperately not to startle her. Judging by the sweetness of her smile, the world of dreams had clearly swept her away, and she looked utterly at peace.

I was overcome by the sheer beauty of the sleeping goddess, her incredibly long auburn hair flowing over the brilliant white pillow onto the bed

The warmth of her body beckoned me; I longed to seek comfort from the howling wind vibrating the window; a constant reminder that winter had not yet passed.

The heat from the sun seemed a far distant memory as I shivered, standing naked on the ice cold floor, convinced as I gazed down at her sleeping image that she could provide all I needed to survive.

I slipped beneath the billowy white duvet, wrapping my arms around her slender body; I could feel her heart beat as I pressed my chest against hers. Would my intrusion frighten her?

Leaning forward, I placed a delicate kiss on her cheek. Her eyes opened, the smile broadening on her lovely face as she welcomed me into her arms . . . and I felt safe.

We kissed passionately as she drew me ever deeper into her warm embrace, igniting a fire within me when I realised that I was in love, captured and bound by a spiritual connection which had until this moment eluded me.

Without thinking I whispered the words, "I love you."

And then . . . she was gone, and I knew that I would never see her again.

[175]

Simon Palmer

RELATIONSHIPS

Where am I going?
What will it be?
What is my fate?
What's waiting for me?

Is there a purpose?
To the pain of the past?
What is the reason?
How long will it last·

Am I a man?
Or still just a shell·

Will I be loved?
Or remain in my hell·

Where is my peace?
Where is my home?
What is a life?
That's destined to roam·

Simon Palmer

There seems to be an overwhelming desire within me to destroy my relationships, the romantic ones are no exception. And I honestly don't know whether any of my shortcomings are a direct result of my childhood experiences, or if I'm just an obnoxious bastard.

I find it impossible to believe anyone can love me. And when I am fortunate enough to find someone, as soon as they begin to get even remotely close, my insecurities take over and I become an unbearable monster to live with, often resorting to verbal, and on a few occasions, physical abuse.

From the time I met the Mother of my Son, to the end of my short lived marriage in February of 2009, and all the relationships between the two, the demons residing within in the darkest corners of my mind have always managed to somehow rob me of the love I hunger for.

Having witnessed first-hand the love my parents shared, my desire to be in a healthy supportive relationship has always been one of my priorities. But I just don't seem to get it right. I know how women should be treated; my Father set an amazing example. I don't remember him raising his voice, much less speaking harshly to my Mum. And she adored him, her eyes lighting up with excitement whenever he stepped through the door. At night, while watching television, my Dad would sit on the floor next to Mum's chair massaging her feet. It never looked to be a chore; he seemed perfectly content just touching her.

[178]

Losing the Hate

I'm not naïve enough to believe the relationship my Parents had was perfect, but it was calm, supportive, and filled laughter.

Even my antics as a teenager failed to create enough friction to break their bond. It was them against me, which is something I resented at the time, but looking back on it now, I am envious . . . truly envious.

And I often find myself wallowing in self pity, true love seems completely unattainable. My demons won't hear of it.

Despite my armour, I do manage to find myself in relationships, and they always start out great, but as my feelings grow, I become convinced I'm going to be hurt. It's never a conscious thing; it's almost as if I've been programmed to self destruct.

The venom that spills from my mouth is poisonous. I once told my ex wife to rot in hell with her dead mother. This is not something I would ever say under normal circumstances, but there's no telling what will set me off once I start feeling threatened.

On this particular night, I just blew up, my aggression rising to such an intense level my wife was forced to leave the house, fearing for her safety. She stayed with a work colleague for the evening, only agreeing to return the following day, once I'd promised to leave.

Feeling absolutely horrid about what I had done, and acknowledging my need for professional help, I made an appointment to see a counsellor. And being the loving person she is, my wife allowed me to move back into our home.

This woman had married me, put up terrible

abuse at my hands, and yet it was still not enough for me to realise she loved me. And it was only a matter of weeks before my next outburst.

Finally, in February of 2009, following a heavy drinking session, I hit her. And quite rightly, she decided it was time to go our separate ways. And wanting what was best for her, I reluctantly agreed.

We were married less than two years.

This is the scenario which has plagued me throughout my adult life. I seem to be incapable of accepting love, to do so feels almost as threatening as being physically attacked. My feelings for a woman seem to unleash the beast within, and no matter how hard I try, I can't seem to control my actions.

I've drifted through a lonely life; my participation in ill-fated relationships has always been somewhat artificial, in the sense of my inability to return the love that's offered. It truly frightens me to think there's a good chance that I will be growing old alone. Perhaps the numerous scars my assailants left on my heart have rendered me emotionally impotent, and if so . . . then they will have effectively stolen my life, not just my childhood, but my entire fucking life.

That being said, there are many people in this world who abuse others and try to excuse their behaviour by blaming the hardships they have endured. And there have been times I have resorted to this cop out myself. But I honestly don't know if my childhood has any bearing on how my personal life has turned out, or if I'm just one of those blokes born to be a bully.

Losing the Hate

Looking in the mirror is sometimes very difficult, and I truly hate myself for the hurt I've caused. It pains me to think there's a whole bunch of women in the world who can only associate bad times when my name is mentioned, each of them having one thought in common; "I wish I'd never met him."

Victim or monster? I just don't know.

Simon Palmer

DRINK AND DRUGS

Once I'd moved into my flat and the rules of Kingfisher were well and truly behind me, my drinking became an issue again, and I began to use cannabis on a daily basis, destroying all I had strived for in a matter of weeks.

I stopped attending work, choosing to "forget" about college, and throwing everyone's support to the wind; as long as I had a spliff and a can of lager in my hand I thought I was happy. The fact that my stomach was always empty, and my bills were going unpaid never crossed my mind. Johnny Rotten was back.

Silence raining down,

Lost within my thoughts,

Self destruction all around·

Lost in a bed-sit,

Demons flooding back,

Enfolded by a darkness,

Shadows cold and black·

Simon Palmer

Crying in a bed-sit,

Ashamed of what I've done,

A hatred for myself,

And all that I've become·

Inevitably, I was once again relying on the social, having just £56 a fortnight to live on and no one for company except my old friend isolation. Visits to my parents' house were always at dinner time, in the hopes my Mother would ask if I wanted to stay.

The time bomb ticking in my head was re-set, but this time it seemed to be scheduled to detonate; the slightest thing sending me into a flying rage.

I'd taken to selling off my property in order to fund my growing habits, and on one occasion I borrowed £30 off of my Father, saying that I needed to buy some clothes for a fictitious job interview, knowing full well I had no way of paying it back. And I went straight down the pub.

Drink and drugs have always dominated my adult life, thinking I needed to use the substances in order to exist, and they acted as means of numbing my emotions. The thought of spending any length of time sober terrifies me, and although I haven't smoked any cannabis for nearly two years, I do still drink far more than is healthy.

During the year of 1995, while living within a homeless unit on the South Coast, not far from Brighton, I met a guy whom I thought was a friend.

[184]

His name was Alex and he introduced me to intravenous drugs.

I'd long since given up my flat to move into a new place with my girlfriend and Son, and after treating them both like shit, moved out of London to stay with my sister, hoping for a new start. It was only a matter of months before the relationship with my sister and brother in law broke down, and I found myself alone yet again . . . as a result of my behaviour . . . yet again.

Moving back to London, I looked up an ex girlfriend and dove head first back into the drug scene, taking LSD most weekends and using dope on a daily basis.

After falling out with one of her friends and having a sawn off shotgun shoved in my face, it was clear I needed to once again get away from the city . . . this time hopefully for good.

Feeling lost and pretty much like a yoyo, I was back on the coast, and lucky enough to have been accepted into a homeless persons unit. This is when things went from bad to worse, in the form of amphetamine sulphate.

Alex and I met in the homeless hostel and it wasn't long before we started sitting on the seafront benches smoking hash. In all honesty I really felt happy; there were no worries of any bills, I was no longer alone within a crowd, and most importantly, I'd met someone who liked me for just being me, or so it seemed.

The social security had given me an emergency payment of around £100 while my claim was being transferred from London, and as the unit supplied all meals, the money was mine to spend, or waste on whatever took my fancy. Alex was kind enough to sort me out some dope, mentioning that he could always get hold of speed; I told him to go for it, handing over more cash. The idea of injecting the stuff never crossed my mind.

When I realised Alex intended to shoot the drug, I was more than a little apprehensive, but not wanting to appear like a coward, I allowed my "mate" to inject my arm. The rush that followed was out of this world, and even before the needle was removed from my arm, I could feel the gear coursing through my entire body. And I wanted to do it again.

The "fix" was etched in my mind, and before long I was shooting up almost   every day, with both food and sleep leaving me, turning my whole being into a shell; I was only living in anticipation of my next rush. It became the best escape from reality I'd ever experienced, and the thoughts of my past magically vanished, suppressing the images of Ropeman, Stuart, and Karen even further into my subconscious.

I became a master at hiding the truth, it was something I'd done all my life, and my drug use was not an exception. Confident all was well in the life of Simon Palmer, my support worker at the unit arranged for me to move into a bedsit.

The injecting continued, and with all of my money being spent on drugs and booze, I'd often attend the local soup kitchen for an afternoon meal, which was where yet another change of lifestyle was waiting for me.

[186]

Losing the Hate

I dropped the friendship with Alex almost immediately, focusing my attentions on the new friend I'd inadvertently discovered at the soup kitchen; a man named Jesus.

I soon realised that an awful lot of the people attending the church I'd joined were also addicts, while I had turned to speed and booze, it was their belief that gave them strength, offering some hope of acceptance at the end of the path which they had chosen to follow. And I wanted desperately to join their chosen path.

I started to go along to group bible studies once a week; and I attended church twice on a Sunday. Before long, I even found myself evangelising at the local High Street. The drug use stopped and my alcohol consumption was cut back to a bare minimum. My new circle of friends encouraged me to visit their houses, often asking me to stay for dinner, and on one occasion taking me along to a Christian rock concert, which I absolutely loved.

However, as with all aspects of my life, whenever things start to head in a more positive direction, my insecurities rear their ugly heads, and I push the good things away, scared that I'm going to be hurt and ripped to shreds.

I pushed the entire group's patience to the very limits, both turning up to their houses blind drunk, as well as high on one chemical or another.

In the beginning they were all very supportive, trying to understand what was going on in my, once again, destructive world. But understandably, none of them were willing to accept my actions for a prolonged period of time, and while they explained I'd always be made to feel welcome at church. I would no longer be welcome to attend group meetings, and invitations to visit their homes were definitely a thing of the past.

I didn't recognize that their reactions were my own doing, and as always, I convinced myself it would have happened anyway. For me, it was just more evidence that people were out to hurt me.

My old friends were back; just Simon, alcohol, and drugs. And I continued to socialise with them, not recognising the harm they were causing, and in truth, if I had, probably wouldn't have cared.

Satan within me,

Satan outside me,

Leave me alone,

Please don't condemn me·

You are a power,

You are a force,

But when you're gone,

I'll feel no remorse·

Like a slug on some salt,

You'll shrivel away,

The darkness will rise,

Right out of the day·

ANGER AND VIOLENCE

There are demons in my head,
Gnawing at my brain,
Torturing my soul,
Driving me insane·
There are demons in my head,
Tearing at my mind,
Devouring my spirit,
Sending shivers down my spine·

Just as in my teenage years, adulthood has seen me stomping through life with nothing but an angry cloud above my head. Using my fists to solve any problems that happen to come my way; it was always an easy option. Rather than looking at a situation rationally, and working things out in a peaceful manner, I continued to fly the handle, hurling threats of violence whenever even slightly frustrated. And I didn't care what people thought of me in the heat of the moment.

[189]

Simon Palmer

The first time my violent threats became physical was with the Mother of my Son, who I shall refer to as Julie. Even before he was born, whenever the two of us argued, often over something trivial, I'd shout and scream, threatening to break her legs, or smash her face in.

As with all domestic abuse, the threats soon became a reality, and when I began to rage there was nothing I could do to stop myself. No matter how badly I felt, or how many promises I'd made, it continued.

Julie loved me to bits, she and I met at Kingfisher, and although the abuse was still fresh in my mind, there's no excuse for the way I treated her. I began to hit her on a regular basis, often going out of my way to create a situation which would give me an excuse to storm out of the flat and go get blind drunk down the pub.

This continued throughout our three years together, but my anger did seem more contained once my son was born, albeit short lived.

As I grew older, instead of the anger and aggression subsiding, it grew to heights which should have scared me to death, but didn't, and I made no connection with the pattern beginning to emerge. It was always everyone else's fault when things went wrong, often with horrific consequences. The self harming became a slight problem again, but it only happened when I was blind drunk, and the wounds were only superficial.

There seemed to be a need for me to project the image of a hard nut; a hooligan with no regard for anyone who didn't fit in. And even today I find myself still on the battlefield with this way of thinking, but things do seem to be getting better.

I've often thought, my life could have been so much happier if I'd had a normal childhood, but, in the cold light of day, can I continue to blame the abuse for the things I've done?

Simon Palmer

MY SON

6th August *1988· 10·50*pm

Lewisham hospital, South London

I had every intention of being the best Father in the world. The love I felt for him the instant he was born was something I had never experienced before . . . and nothing has overwhelmed me to that degree since. Apart from the actual birth, one of my fondest memories of the evening was when Julie, with our baby cuddled in her arms, said to me, "Come and meet your son."

In my minds eye I can still see his little screwed up face; the sound of his first cries in the world still ring in my eardrums. And once I held him in my arms all that mattered was the love I felt for him, and I vowed in earnest to protect the young beautiful life I'd helped create.

And I failed him.

[193]

Aside from going to work, I put absolutely no effort into providing my child, whom we had named James, a loving family environment. In fact, all I managed to contribute was pain and heartache.

While Julie was busy at home looking after baby James, I continued my drunken nights out down the pub, having affairs with young dolly birds, spending what should have been my Son's money on buying them drinks and cigarettes.

The physical abuse towards his Mother became more and more horrendous by the day, but I believed it was justified; it was I who was the one being hard done by. When I think of the times I used to slag Julie off to my parents, claiming she wouldn't even bother to cook for me and ranting about her inability to keep a clean house embarrasses me to this day.

I was an evil young man with no feeling for anyone but myself.

One terrible occasion will always stick in my mind. It was a Sunday afternoon, Julie and I had decided to go to the local park where there was a bit of a Fete taking place. And so with James in the pushchair, we walked the short journey to the celebrations. We'd arranged to meet a friend of ours, Laura, at the main entrance, and intended to make a day of it, strolling around the various stalls.

We had not anticipated that there would be a beer tent.

"Look. There's only a fuckin' bar." I exclaimed, already shoving my hand in my pocket, hoping I had enough cash on me.

[194]

"D'you have to," asked Julie, rolling her eyes,"you've got plenty of cans back home; we won't be here that long."

I glared at her, "Shut the fuck up." And with that fond farewell, I disappeared into the crowd. Pushing my way to the trestle table, I waved a ten pound note in the air, franticly trying to grab the barman's attention, as if my very life depended on it.

Getting very impatient, I leaned as far across the makeshift bar as was physically possible and shouted for service; more than a few heads turning in my direction as I did so. The guy behind the table finally looked at me, an expression of total contempt etched on his face, but he served me just the same. After paying for the glass of cloudy beer, I scanned the area to see if I recognised anyone. My body froze, and the glass I was holding threatened to shatter under the pressure. It was Ropeman, fuck me, it was Ropeman!

The first thoughts entering my mind were extremely violent. It would take no effort at all to drive my glass into his throat; to twist and turn it until every last drop of his poisonous blood drained from his lifeless body. I imagined a bloodstained corpse sprawled on the grass; saw myself kicking and punching the putrid remains until the police arrived and arrested me for the cold blooded murder of a "respected"school teacher.

Finding it very difficult to contain myself, I walked towards him, not quite knowing what I intended to do. He began smiling that same old pathetic smile of his, trying to look as if he was happy to see me, but I saw through him; the look of terror apparent in his soulless eyes.

At the last minute, my thoughts reversed. It wasn't fear, far from it; in reality I could easily snap his neck. For whatever reason, it became more important that he see, despite what he'd done, I had survived. Although this was far from being true, outwardly it would appear I was doing well.

"Hello Simon, I don't believe it. How the devil are you?"

"Yeah, I'm fuckin' great, you?" I gulped at my drink.

"Not too bad, I'm teaching at a different school these days, the pay rise helps too."

(And how many little boys' lives have you destroyed since working there?)

It was clear he didn't want to talk, as his next sentence confirmed, "Anyway, it's nice to see you, but I must get on. You look after yourself, ok?"

Tilting my glass in his direction, I nodded goodbye and he was gone, leaving me every bit as empty and violated as the last time I'd seen him all those years ago.

I needed another drink.

After downing four or five pints of real ale, I decided to go in search of Julie and Laura; feeling an immediate need to be free of the crowd which was suffocating me from all directions.

And my anger was rising.

[196]

Losing the Hate

I don't know you,
An' you don't know me,
Get out of my way,
Just leave me be·
I'll tear you apart,
Limb from limb,
An' all the while,
I'll imagine you're him·
Give me an excuse,
An' I'll destroy you're life,
Slash your throat,
Kill your wife
Stamp on your head,
'Till your skull caves in,
An' all the while,
I'll imagine you're him·
Murder you all,
An' imagine you're him·

It wasn't long before I was pushing through a throng of mums and dads. Everyone busy laughing as their children ran around screaming and shouting with delight at the many sideshows on offer.

And my anger's still rising.

[197]

After completing two circuits of the madness and mayhem surrounding me, I decided to go back to the beer tent; thinking they may have been trying to find me.

And my anger was rising.

"Simon. Over here!" They were sitting on a bench outside the toilets.

"Where the fuck do you think you've been?" I bellowed, causing people to look in my direction for the second time that day.

The finale of that terrible afternoon saw me kick my child's pushchair over, and punch Julie in the side of the head twice; my Son was in her arms at the time.

As if that wasn't bad enough, once I'd returned home, and with my temper still raging, I completely trashed the lounge, destroying everything I could get my hands on, which included James' toys.

If I'd heard of someone else acting in such a despicable manner, I would have one simple word befitting such a person; scum. Anyone in their right mind knows behaviour like that is beyond unacceptable, it is the lowest of the low, and there are no excuses to defend such horrific actions.

I've not been in James' life since he was four years old, and it hurts me far more than any of the evil acts I was subjected to. I've missed out on so much; kicking a football in the park, helping him with homework, enjoying the look on his face Christmas morning . . . so many lost years, times that no amount of wishing can bring back.

Losing the Hate

Often there are simply no second chances. This is something I've found out the hard way; the way I discover most things, by fucking them up beyond belief.

And in truth, when it comes to James most especially, I'm not deserving of a second chance. What bothers me most is that my Son is paying the consequences for my selfish acts. He was the one cheated, and I got exactly what I deserved.

On numerous occasions I've taken steps to find my Son, but I always seem to come up against a brick wall.

However, if I'm truly honest, I certainly could've done more, an awful lot more.

I miss him so terribly much.

Simon Palmer

DROPPING THE SWORD

In many ways the experiences I've had as an adult, have been far worse than the abuse I suffered at the hands of those monsters so many years ago. It's tragic that I was unlucky enough to come into contact with them, but they would have found another child in place of me . . . and because of my silence, they probably did anyways. But I cannot continue to dwell on this thought, it has eaten me from the inside out for far too long.

Nothing would give me more satisfaction than having the opportunity to ask them all one simple question . . . Why? But let's face it; I doubt I'd get an honest answer.

It's not a trade off by any means, but were it not for those horrid early experiences I may have never discovered my love of writing. And the realisation that I, a man who admittedly has hung on by the thinnest of threads for most of my life, may have at least been given just enough talent to speak out for the voiceless.

[201]

Simon Palmer

Not only on behalf of the innocent children subjected to unspeakable acts of depravity, but also for the adult survivors, who were at one time every bit as innocent, and continue to be blameless.

I'm hoping my writing **Losing the Hate**, will help me come to terms with my experiences too. But in my case, it is not so much the things that were done to me which cause me the most distress anymore, it's the way I chose (or neglected) to deal with them.

For many years material possessions were very important to me, however, I have come to realise, a contented life is by far more valuable, and in terms of happiness the smile of a loved one brings an inner peace which cannot be found in deepest of wallets.

My adult life has taken me down many different and often painful roads, all of which overshadowed by the ghosts of my many mistakes. Time and time again, I have walked away from situations with nothing more than the clothes on my back; always leaving behind the possessions I'd worked so hard for. Shamefully often missing the objects far more than people I knew would never be a part of my life again. In hindsight, I can barely recall my belongings, but I think of the people quite often.

There has only been one constant in my life, one companion who has remained faithful and accompanied me on my many journeys. Through the good times it has been my rock, and I have used it as my crutch when life seemed to be doing its damnedest to destroy me. My writing has kept me sane, specifically my poetry.

[202]

Losing the Hate

Through the passage of time, my soul has cried out to write. It's a fact most of the verses flowing from my pen are of a very dark nature. But it reflects my thoughts, the ones continuously infusing my brain, so rather than deny their existence I allow them to flourish.

There is so much of my early life I'd like to forget, but I really don't believe forgetting is the answer. In order to truly move on, I've found it necessary not to lose sight of the things that have hindered me in the past, for only then can I move on to the next chapter.

During the times I find myself reflecting, I've taken to reading my writings, transporting myself back in time, back to the poetry which has helped ease so many of my burdens.

Although, I strongly believe my life would have turned out differently if the abuse had not taken place, in my experience the only way to move forward is to let go of the past.

My goal at this point is to live the rest of my life as an example for others. At very least, I'd like to be remembered as "the man who changed," as opposed to "that man."

As I've said, I genuinely feel partly responsible for any further atrocious acts of indecency my violators may have committed. If I could go back in time, their well-deserved prison sentences would most certainly be served. But at this point I have to place my faith in a higher power to exact my revenge, because frankly the war I have been waging has been against myself.

The constant abuse I've subjected my body to over the years with one substance or another has left me with stomach ulcers, emphysema, and high blood pressure which I have to take daily medication for. My arms are a mass of scars from the extreme wounds I've inflicted on myself.

I did not include a great deal of information on my self-harming, but it was a constant in my life for many years, so I thought I would at least touch on the subject.

This is by no means an attempt to explain the dynamics of self-harming. I don't understand it myself, but I'll share how I experienced it.

There have been many times in my life when the sensation of angry ants crawling just below the surface of my skin threatened to drive me mad. It felt as though they were gnawing at my skin, ready to devour my flesh. The feeling that I was being eaten from the inside out is the best way I can describe it. There seemed to be no relief . . . just an endless assault by invisible enemies declaring war from within my own body.

As these horrible feelings intensified, the stronger the urge to hurt myself became. It was as if the wounds I inflicted on my body were actually enabling the creatures dwelling beneath my skin to escape, leaving me temporarily relieved.

I have taken razorblades, broken beer bottles, and even lighters to my arms, desperately trying to rid myself of the sensation. In hindsight, I believe these were feelings, emotions which I chose to suppress, memories that can only be pushed so far back into ones mind, before they push back, with a vengeance.

Losing the Hate

My self-harming has never been an attempt at suicide, and it wasn't attention seeking. It was just a means of relieving the constant emotional torment.

These actions were at their height during my time at Kingfisher, but there was an occasion when I literally hacked at myself with a razorblade whilst aimlessly wandering through a busy shopping centre in South London. The result was over 200 hundred stitches, ironically these actions only served to fuel my self-hatred, which in turn, made me want to do something similar in order to ease the new pain.

It was vicious cycle, which at time seemed impossible to break.

Whenever the blood flowed from inside me, I felt a great sense of relief, and there were many times when watching it actually made me feel content, like I had accomplished something.

There was never any great battle within me to stop doing it, in fact, I often looked forward to the feeling of self gratification in hurting myself; it was the only thing that appeared to ease my pain.

As I grew older, the need to do these things were alleviated, until finally, thankfully, it became nothing more than another bad installment of my complex past.

I've often heard people expressing anger at those who self harm. I personally think these views aren't altogether justified. Very few things are black and white, and when it comes to admonishing someone for these actions, in my experience, it only serves to escalate the problem. It's very much like scratching an unbearable itch.

Simon Palmer

In the present, I try to hide my many scars by wearing long sleeves whenever possible, and I have numerous tattoos to cover the more drastic damage. Having said that, on the many occasions that I've been asked how they came to be, I have always been honest, and I feel no shame in telling others that the scars were self-inflicted.

Am I the same as you?
When will I die?
There are so many questions,
Tell me, who am I·
I think all the time,
So many things I try,
I know I've found a skill,
But tell me, who am I·
Do I have a label?
Or is my life a sham?
Maybe if I try,
I'll find out who I am·

Losing the Hate

I wish that my parents had been able to enjoy my teenage years and see me do well at school or even university, but I did manage to make my peace with them before they sadly passed away, Dad going in *1997*, with Mum joining him in *2001*.

    I will always love the both of them from the bottom of my heart, and I'm sure that, despite all I've done, they're both looking down at me, smiling and feeling quite proud.

Sye Palmer

Simon Palmer

CPSIA information can be obtained
at www.ICGtesting.com
Printed in the USA
FSOW01n1738310716
23287FS